YOU KNIT UNIQUE

YOU KNIT
Unique

Inspiration and Information
for the Original Knitter

Lee Andersen

First published 1985

Special edition for Softly 1986
Second edition 1989
Third edition 1992
Copyright 1985 Lee Andersen

ISBN 0-9629520-1-X

Published by Eagle-Anderson
Eagle USA
P.O. Box 48282
Seattle, Washington 98166

Printed in Hong Kong
By Kings Time Printing Press Ltd.

CONTENTS

Other books by Lee Andersen

EXTRA- Ordinarily You

Coat and sweater patterns for all women, with special emphasis on flattering the fuller figure.

You and Yours

Contemporary sweater patterns for men (and their female friends).

Reflections of You

Designer sweater patterns for children (with adult sizes given) and full instructions on knitting from a child's drawings or other masterpieces.

The Casual You

Fifty-one contemporary outdoor coat and sweater patterns from twenty-seven designs for the entire family.

The Original Knitter's Design Kit

Sixteen extra large sheets of graph paper complete with standard sweater shapes in four different sizes plus a tension square and guidelines.

All Lee Andersen books and yarns available through
Eagle U S A
P.O. Box 48282
Seattle, Washington. 98166

Lee Andersen

Lee is a New Zealander with a talented knitter for a mother.
She was brought up believing a house full of colourful yarn was normal and that knitting was just
something that came off the needles. Her mother knitted whatever was necessary for the constantly
accumulating children around her. (Lee is one of six and now there are grand children ...)

After completing a Bachelor of Education majoring in Art and a three year Diploma of Teaching, Lee
began painting and exploring wearable art and, naturally, knitting surfaced as a medium.

When the designs started coming faster than her fingers could knit she began working with other knitters
in New Zealand until over 100 of the best were working straight from her drawings.

Her gallery Vibrant Handknits in Wellington, New Zealand supplied "one only " garments to "the rich,
the famous and the royal" from around the world for six years.

Then in 1988 Lee fell in love! Unfortunately, Al lived in a different country (the U.S.) and knitting
needles and coloured pencils are mobile. Lee moved.

Her first book "You Knit, Unique" teaches knitters how to design and offers humourous but practical
solutions to those inevitable mishaps.

This book belongs to a series of 20 pattern books for those knitters who want to knit a specific garment but
still want suggestions for altering colour and sizes.

INTRODUCTION

The potential of knitting is unlimited. All knitters around the world are conscious of its soothing and rewarding nature. We are becoming aware, also, that the craft lends itself to the expression of more personal and even extreme statements than can be expressed by following traditional patterns.

My mother taught me to delight in wool and knitting and to use it to achieve my own ends. Any patterns in the house were there for ideas, stitch numbers or to be used as coffee coasters! Her knitting philosophy has had an extended influence on my life, and I'd like to impart it to you.

By its very nature, this cannot be a book of patterns. Its purpose is to give you the confidence to use the craft of knitting as you see fit, to create a garment or an object that is personally yours, from the colours and textures of the yarns to the shape of the neckline.

The technical information, illustrations and ideas provided in the chapters that follow are intended to give you what you need to make personal choices boldly, knowing that they will work: but don't feel bound by what is in this book. The fact that it is published and presented between beautiful covers doesn't make it necessarily right, the best or only way. Hopefully, it will whet your appetite and encourage you to ask or look for further information or, better still, experiment yourself.

This book is a kind of salve. I have to admit to an ambivalent response to others who design and create wonderful pieces I wish I had made myself. By encouraging you, to the very best of my ability, to create beautiful and exciting original knitwear, I hope to feel a kinship with any knitted treasures you make. Quite apart from that, YOU KNIT UNIQUE is an expression of my pride in the creative ability of my fellow New Zealanders and my deep love of knitting, colour, wool and sheep — the ones with the fluffy cheeks, especially!

I dedicate this book, YOU KNIT UNIQUE,
to my mother, Colleen Wilson,
"who taught me everything I know . . ."

CHAPTER ONE

COLOUR

Colour affects our moods, our appearance and, some would say, our state of health. It is even written in our language of feelings — a blue mood, green with envy, a red-letter day. Many books have been written on the psychology of colour, but essentially each colour evokes a feeling.

Red is an action colour, warm, alive and full of energy. Blue is more gentle, passive and cool. Pink is feminine and disarming. Purple is royal, while green and brown are more earthbound. Yellow can be young and positive, or intellectual.

There's more to colour than meets the eye, and a good feel for colour or knowledge of colour theory is a great asset to knitters and, in fact, anyone making or choosing garments of any kind. The information in this chapter is intended to introduce the subject gently and hopefully inspire you to create knitted masterpieces in which the colours sing, evoke a certain mood or reflect the personality of the wearer.

If you already have in mind a particular colour range and yarn for your next project, skip this section and go on to the chapter on design. If, on the other hand, you are feeling confused, befuddled or indecisive, read on.

PRIMARY COLOURS

The primary colours are red,
yellow and blue. They are the
three colours that cannot be
made by mixing together other
colours. They are powerful and
bright and usually well loved
by children and the young at
heart.

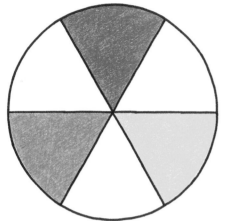

SECONDARY COLOURS

The secondary colours, purple,
orange and green, are made by
combining two of the primary
colours. Red and blue
combined make purple. Red
and yellow combined make
orange. Yellow and blue
combined make green.

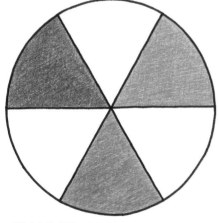

SHADES AND TINTS

Shades are colours that have
been subdued by the addition
of black. Pastels and tints are
colours that have been
lightened by the addition of

*Pastel bobble jersey using only tints
photographed by More.*

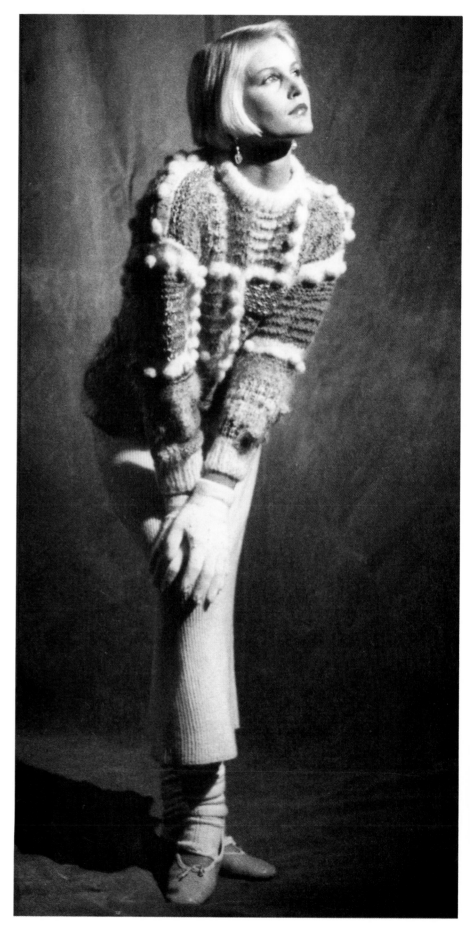

10

white. Sometimes the terms "shade" and "tint" are used in general conversation to describe any colour at all, but the above definitions are the technically correct ones when dealing with colour theory. If you become familiar with them it will be helpful when referring to art books or books on dyeing methods.

The accompanying diagram shows the tints and shades that result from the addition of black and white to the primary and secondary colours.

MONOCHROMATIC COLOUR RANGES

You may choose to use in your knitting only tints and/or shades of one colour instead of a variety of colours. This is a safe way of working if you are still unsure of your sense of colour. It works well in textured knitting (see Chapter 4), allowing the different textures and yarn weights to be the focal point of the knitting.

A twelve step colour wheel showing tints (white added) and shades (black added). Mary Hazlewood's Baby Blue cotton jersey using only shades and tints of blue.

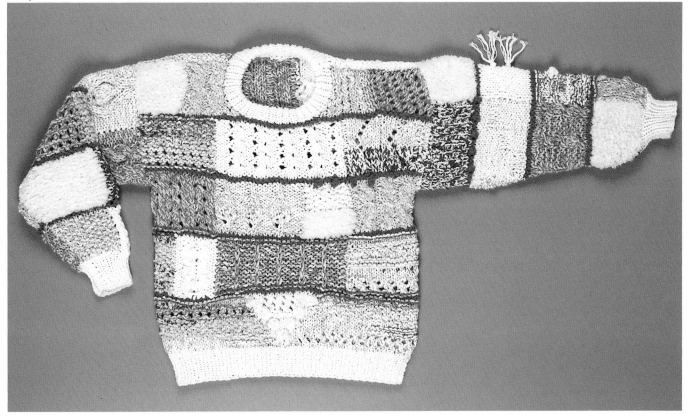

Tonally matched yarns become evident in a black and white photo.   TC

TONALLY MATCHED COLOUR RANGES

A tonally matched colour range is one that includes a variety of colours that are all of a similar tone (that is, darkness or brightness). The areas marked by circles in the diagram are all tonally matched. Tonally matched colours always look right together and can be relied upon to work in a design that is very complex or erratic and in garments that include a wide range of textures, stitches and types of yarn. Tonally matched colour ranges seem to hold a design together.

In some cases (for instance, if your design is a "picture") it may not be possible to limit the colours to a single range of tones. Then, you may choose to work with more than one tonal range with complete justification.

If you find it hard to decide whether two colours or hues are tonally matched, try squinting your eyes to block out most of the light. If one colour is much lighter or darker than the other, the effect will be exaggerated and more easy to see.

To test this technique, look at a wall or column that is painted a single colour but is shaded on one side. If you squint your eyes the difference between the light and dark areas will seem to leap out at you.

Alternatively, take a black and white photograph of the two yarns you wish to test. This method is effective but time consuming and difficult to explain to the family!

PURE COLOUR VERSUS EARTHY COLOUR

Another safe practice is to limit a design to either all pure colours or all earthy colours, as shown in the accompanying photograph. You may experiment with confidence within this limitation, but it is relatively difficult to combine colours from both groups successfully. One exception (you will probably find others) is the use of pure highlights, especially red, in an overall earthy range of colours.

TC

Earthy red, orange and yellow on the left and pure red, orange and yellow on the right.

COMPLEMENTARY COLOURS

Despite their name, complementary colours are not colours that say nice things to people. They are, in fact, colours that are positioned opposite each other on the colour wheel. The arrangement of colours on such a wheel was not the result of an arbitrary decision on the part of early writers of art books, but instead recognition of the fact that certain colours seem to complement each other, or make each other whole.

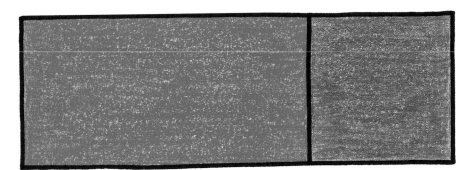

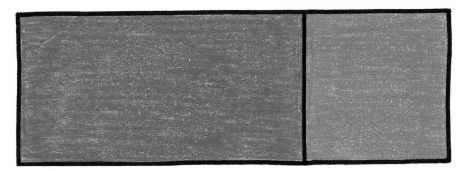

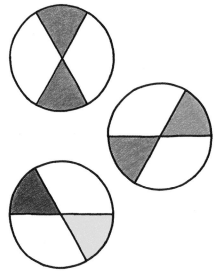

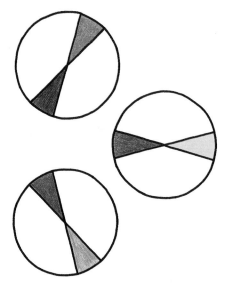

If you stare at a single colour for a minute or so, then shut your eyes quickly, the complementary colour will appear on your eyelids as an after image. Experienced complementary colour catchers can stare at a colour, then look at a plain wall and see the complementary after image.

When complementary colours are placed next to each other in a design they enhance each other. Touches of the complementary colour to the main colour in a design brighten up the main colour. If the main colour is green, touches of red will liven it up. A main colour of purple will be excited by touches of yellow, and blue will be enhanced by orange.

Complementaries do not necessarily have to be pure primary colours and their opposite secondary colours on the wheel. Every shade or tint has a complementary colour, and many complementary combinations are subtly dramatic, if there is such a thing. For instance, the complementary of a tomato or reddy orange is a blue-green. The complementary of indigo is a pumpkin orange and, to retain the edible imagery, the complementary of reddy purple is lime.

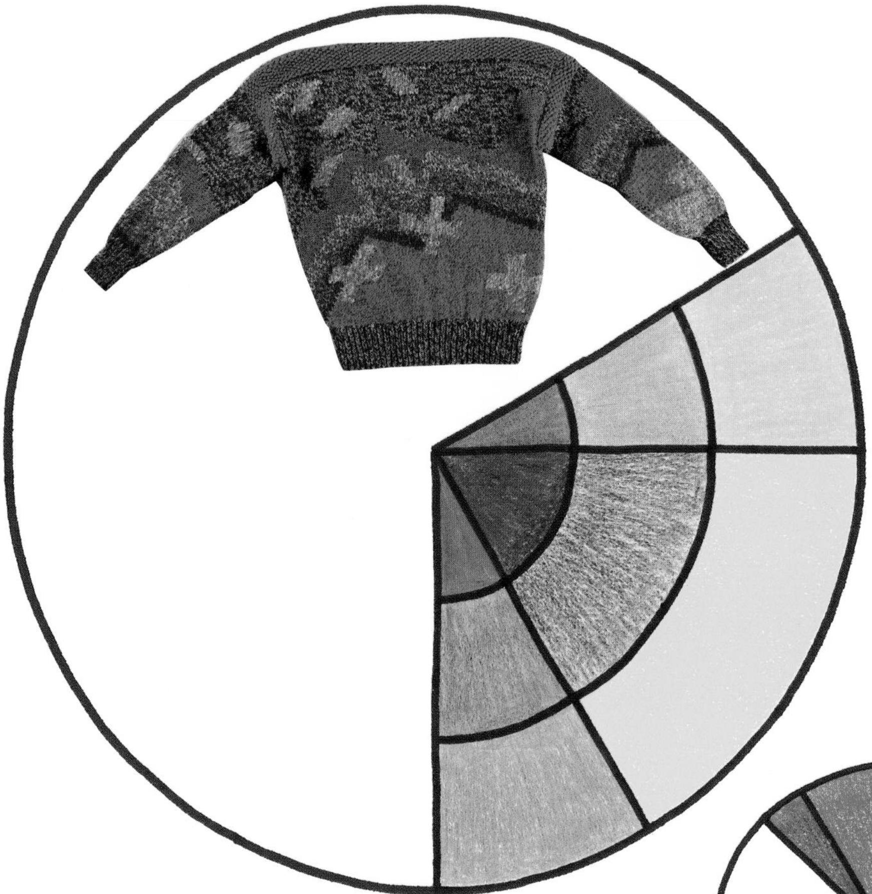

COMBINATIONS

When working with a three-colour analogous or harmonious set, try adding a small amount of the complementary of the central colour to give extra life to the design. These are shown in the accompanying diagrams.

If you're using only two colours of an analogous set and wish to add a touch of the appropriate complementary, it will be the colour directly opposite the dividing line between the two analogous colours.

Above left: Orange crosses travel from the analogous red to the complementary blue in this garment creating a feeling of the crosses originating in the red and moving out into a contrasting world. **Above:** A colour wheel showing the analogous colours with the primary base of yellow.

ANALOGOUS COLOURS

Analogous colours are those that are close to each other on the colour wheel. Their name derives from the word analogy, meaning a reference to some likeness between two objects or events. Analogous colours are like each other in that they contain the same primary colour as a base. They tend to work well together in a garment.

To help you remember the difference between the terms complementary and analogous, think of complementary colours as being contrasting, like two people standing opposite each other and complimenting each other in a conversation. Analogous colours are like siblings, brothers and sisters, with some common element. We'll call the brothers and sisters Anne, Al and Gus (analogous).

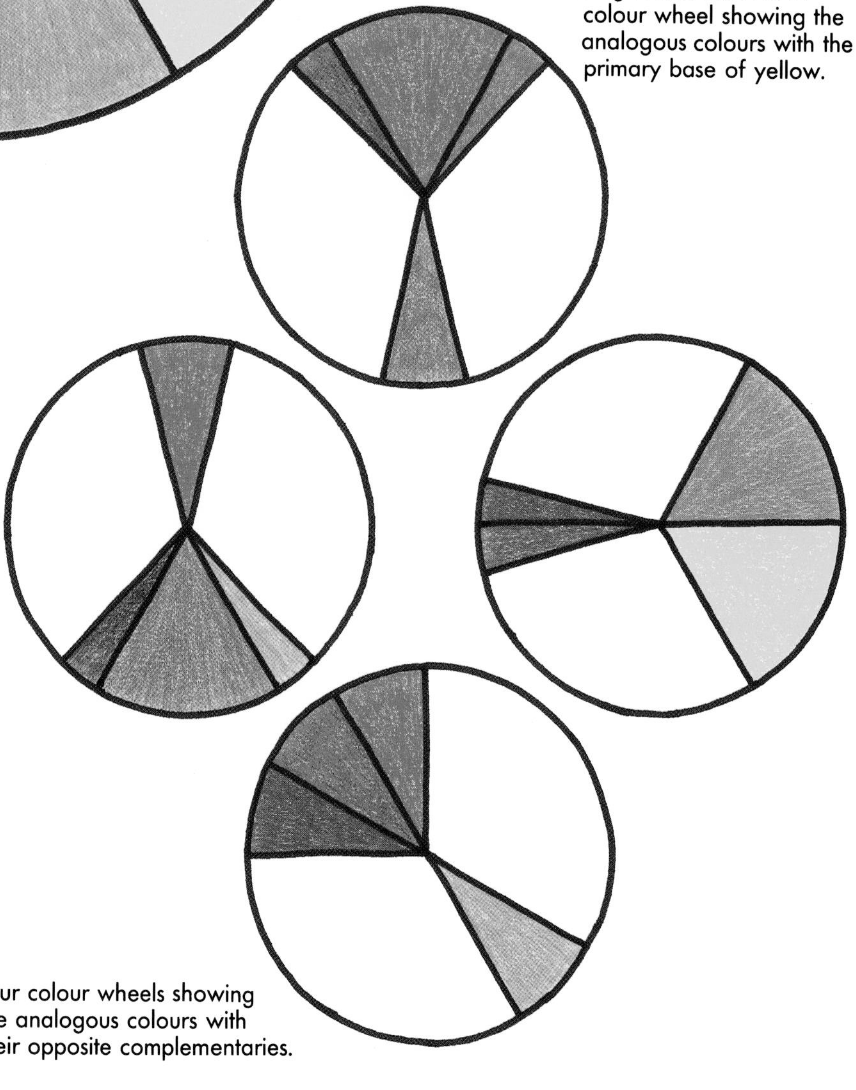

Four colour wheels showing the analogous colours with their opposite complementaries.

Right: The warm yellow attracts the eye away from the cool blue.

COLOUR LEADS THE EYE

The properties of colour can be used to advantage in a garment to focus attention away from height and weight problems. By the careful placement of colours you can make the wearer appear thinner or taller. It's certainly easier than dieting!

Tints and warm colours (reds, pinks, golds, for instance) appear to come forward, attracting attention and making the area they cover seem larger. Keeping these colours to the centre of the body and away from "problem areas" will flatter most figure shapes.

Shades and cool colours (blues, dark greys and blue-greys, blue-greens and blue-purples, for instance) appear to sink into the background and make the area they cover seem smaller. By using these at the sides of the body and over areas you would rather play down, attention will be attracted elsewhere.

For instance, a design with yellow at the neck leading to blue on the bust would lead the eye towards the face. A design with yellow at the bustline and blue at the neck would lead the eye towards the bust. A design with red over the hips and cool colours elsewhere would attract attention to the hips, but a design with cool colours over the hips and red by the face would take attention away from the hips and up to the face.

If your left shoulder is the only spot you like on your whole body, a pink flower placed there would attract attention to it!

COLOUR DECEIVES THE EYE

Colours can be modified or intensified by placing them in juxtaposition with other colours. If blue-green is surrounded with pure green, the blue or odd colour will be intensified. If the surrounding colour is pure blue, the green of the blue-green inside square will be intensified, as shown. A colour surrounded with black will be intensified, whereas a grey surround will have no effect, leaving the colour looking the same.

A thin line of black on a red background may take on a greenish tinge, the complementary of the red. To offset this effect, choose a reddish black for the line as it will be more likely to appear jet black.

The way colour deceives the eye has been researched in depth. More technical information on this subject may be found in art books dealing with the theory of colour.

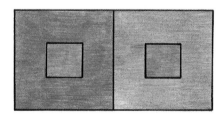

PROPORTIONS OF COLOUR

If you've decided on a main colour and tonal range for your creation, but are still reluctant to commit yourself to a specific design, here's a legitimate excuse for putting off the decision a little longer!

The proportions in which colours are used in a design can have profound effects, as shown in the diagrams opposite. These three samplers all contain the same colours, but in varying amounts, and the results are obvious. The samples shown could be transferred to a general garment design as shown, creating three totally different jerseys.

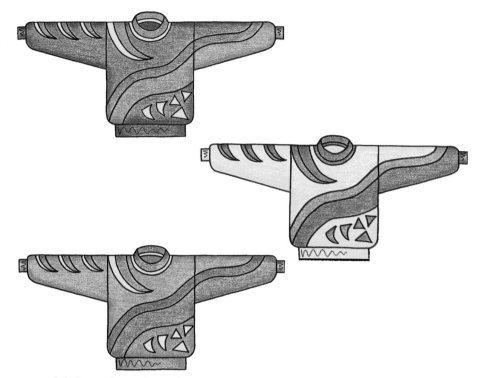

Three optional proportions.   TC

When you've chosen the basic lines of the garment and the number of colours you wish to use, experiment with varying proportions of colour, using scrap paper and coloured pencils. If you already have the yarns, try wrapping them around a strip of card in varying proportions, as in the samples shown. Although these examples contain tonally related colours, the exercise is useful if you have bravely chosen to work in a wide range of tones (dark and light yarns) and colours. It is even more useful if you are designing a large piece such as a rug or a wall hanging.

The following information may be helpful as a general guide when working with a wide range of tones. Choose the largest colour area and establish whether it is dark, medium or light in tone. Let's assume it is dark. Any other colours will be lighter than this or tonally matched. If the other yarns are only slightly lighter in tone they can be used to cover a reasonably wide area without taking over from the main colour. However, if one yarn is much lighter in tone than the main colour it will remain in balance only if it is used in small areas.

Like tints, warm colours — reds, golds, yellows, pinks — may be used in smaller amounts than the cool colours of the spectrum and yet still hold their own in a design.

A small warm pink square highlights natural olives and greys.   TC

PERSONAL COLOUR

Depending on your personal colouring, your hair, eye colour and skin tone, there is a specific range of colours and variations of these that will make you look and feel good when you wear them. These are known as your personal colours and are often described by colour consultants as spring, summer, autumn or winter colours.

Complete books have been written on personal colour, and professional advice from beauty consultants is available for those who wish to explore this subject to the full. However, you may already have an idea of the colours that suit you best and the contents of your wardrobe probably reflect this. Not everyone feels able to wear bright pure hues or black and white — such bold colours may feel overwhelming. Tints, shades or earthy combinations may be more appropriate.

In the field of personal colour there is still a wide range of choices because of the infinite variations of each colour. For instance, blue can be anything from a cool grey-blue or greenish blue to a warm purply-blue containing a touch of red. A pink containing a touch of blue has a mauve feel about it, and it is a cool colour when compared to a pink containing a touch of yellow. Your personal colour range may include cool pinks and blues, but omit honey pink.

The warmth or coolness of a secondary colour may be affected at a more basic level by the "temperature" of the primary colours used as its base. For instance, reds may tend towards blue (cool) or yellow (warm), affecting the types of purples and oranges that may be made with them.

TC

A winter personal colouring
An autumn personal colouring

TC

Dyed yarns wrapped into a colour wheel.

DYEING YOUR OWN YARN

Many handspinners dye their own wool with wonderful results. Commercially spun yarns can also be dyed successfully. Both natural and chemical dyes are available and the choice of which to use is a personal one.

Natural dyes, from plant material, are time consuming to use but immensely satisfying. Chemical dyes are quick and efficient. I use Panhue and Ciba dyes for colouring wool and mohair and find them quite exhilarating to use and challenging enough for me. I suspect that if I became involved in natural dyeing I would become hooked on it, forever seeking out a new colour from an untried plant. If *you* wish to explore the field of natural dyeing, further information may be found at your library and spinners and weavers guilds.

Ciba and Panhue dyes are available in pure colours, but pastels and tints can be dyed by omitting the ascetic acid which normally increases the uptake of the dye. Generally, however, the yarn still needs to be heated for the full length of time specified.

If you have children in the house, it may be safer to use larger doses of white vinegar instead of ascetic acid. After all, it can be used on your fish and chips as well! However, don't eat or prepare food while you are dyeing yarn. Regardless of how much fun they are to use, chemical dyes are poisonous.

Home dyeing is a wonderful way of obtaining uniquely coloured yarns, which are an asset to any original knit. The colour variations that can be achieved are infinite. In the illustration opposite, the gradations of colour have been achieved by gently introducing a touch more of the neighbouring primary colour until the whole spectrum has been covered.

Primaries dictate secondaries
Depending on the type of red, blue and yellow dye you have, it is possible to mix greens, oranges, purples and lots of browns. Clean, bright secondary colours can be dyed by mixing together pure primary hues.

If you are having difficulty mixing a particular secondary colour, I suggest you check the primaries being used. Your red could actually be an orange-red which, when mixed with blue, will yield only a muddy purple, not a royal purple. If you want grass green but your greens tend towards khaki, check the purity of your yellow. It may well be a golden yellow containing a small amount of red pigment.

Dyeing a hank that is already coloured provides interesting results. (This usually works only with a lightly coloured hank.) A hank that is already bluish will tend to yield

Jan Macdonald's hand-dyed mohair jersey.

Plum and Ochre jersey, designed and knitted by Lee Andersen.

medium-strength colour, while blue is the strongest. It is a good idea to take this into account when mixing colours, to avoid overpowering weak colours in a mixture. If possible, add blue to yellow to make green, not the other way around. If you try to make green by adding yellow to blue you may use up the whole container of yellow without affecting the blue!

The "Plum and Ochre Scribble" jersey shown in the

mauve-pinks, blue-greens, greeny yellows or earthy oranges, depending on the colour of the new dye used. A hank that is already brownish will cause any colour dyed over it to become earthy. Such results can be used to advantage by dyeing all the colours to be used in a garment over already dyed matching hanks. This will give all the yarns a common background, ensuring that they go well together.

Dyeing with complementaries

Wonderful, earthy colours *can* be dyed with chemical dyes simply by adding a touch of black or, better still, a touch of the complementary or opposite colour to the main colour.

If a bright red yarn seems to be overpowering the other

colours in your design, pop it in a dyebath with a touch of green dye. This will knock back the intensity of the red without killing it or making it look dirty, as black dye can sometimes do. If, on the other hand, you have a lime green yarn that seems to glow in the dark, a tiny amount of red dye will make it slightly khaki green. Add only a very small amount of red first and increase the dosage if it has no effect on the intensity of the green.

This brings us to the question of the *strength* of various colours. Yellow is the most delicate colour and can be changed by adding miniscule amounts of a stronger colour. Red is a

photograph here is an example of the results that can be obtained by dyeing with complementary colours. The original intention was to create a dramatic yellow and purple scribble pattern. It started with a wool dyed bright yellow (as in the cross on the sleeve) and some natural grey fleece which I intended to dye bright purple. However, after dyeing, it came out a browny-plum colour, which clashed horribly with the bright yellow . . . but colour theory to the rescue! Straight into the leftover purple dye went all but one of the bright yellow hanks, and the result was a rich ochre colour that went well with the browny-plum.

There is an exact combination of complementary colours that makes grey, but the number of browns that can be made this way is much greater and more likely to be the result. The outcome of mixing complementary colours is affected by the proportions of complementary colours used. The difficulty with this technique is achieving the knack of subduing colours with their complementaries without ending up with 2,000 different browns.

In a nutshell, brown is the result of mixing all three primary colours. It is also the result of mixing a primary and its opposite secondary colour, which is actually the same thing.

This deep armholed waistcoat and matching batwing jersey show a range of greys diagonally crossing other blended colours. This subtly changes the relationship between the variables.

Browns in simple relationships to other colours photographed by *More*.

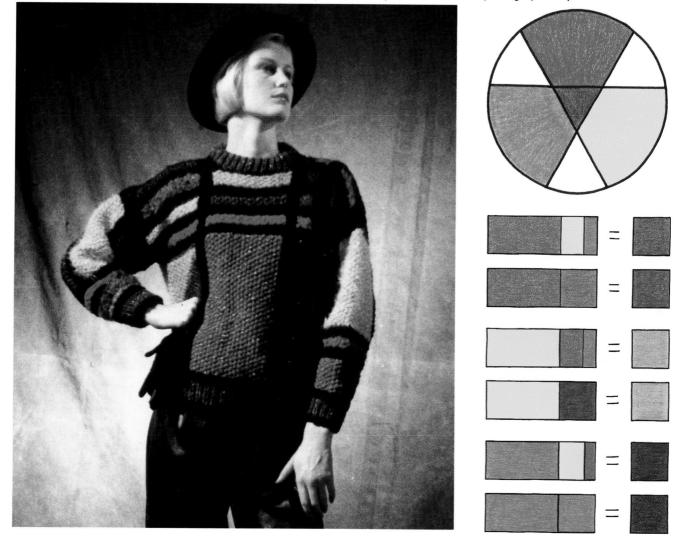

Dyeing a rainbow hank A rainbow-coloured hank of yarn can be made by random dip-dyeing as follows:

Wind white or light-coloured yarn into a large hank (the longer the hank, the easier it is to achieve the rainbow effect). Prepare three dyepots, each containing one of the primary colours, red, blue and yellow. Put different parts of the hank into each dyepot, as shown, and follow the instructions on the dye containers for dyeing parts of the hank in each of the primary colours. When this process is complete, shift the position of the hank so that the undyed areas are sitting in the dye and some of the already dyed areas are overdyed with another primary colour. The overdyed areas will take on a secondary colour, green, orange, or purple, depending on which two dyes were combined in those areas. Voila — a rainbow hank!

This type of hank often knits up best in a simple textured stitch such as reverse stocking stitch, garter stitch or moss stitch. Amazing variations in colour that quite confound the viewer can be obtained by knitting two rainbow or random-dyed hanks together.

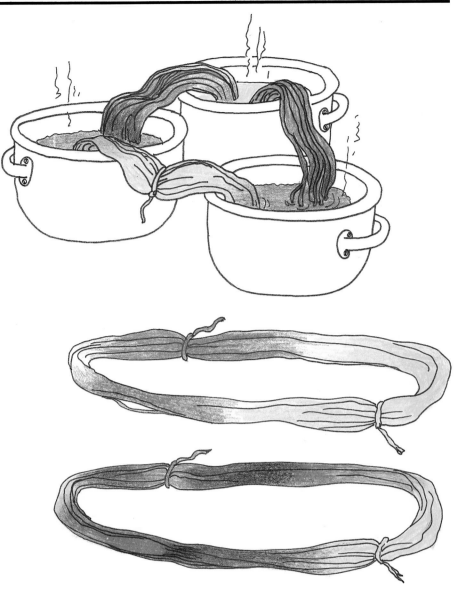

Paua shell jersey incorporating random dip-dyed handspun wool designed and knitted by Lee Andersen.

A relatively tight colour range (blues, mauves and pinks) is held together by a black background in this batwing cardigan designed on the needles by Lee Andersen.   TC

The clear light and sharp contrasts of New Zealand contribute the pink/orange and blue/green, black and white of this design.   TC

CHAPTER TWO

DESIGN

Let me begin with an anecdote which typifies my approach to knitting and design, which is not as formal an affair as you might think.

One sunny day, as I was walking along the street near my shop I saw, to my despair, a wonderful jersey that I hadn't created coming towards me. It was striped and tigerish, in yellow, black and red. The distance between us was sufficient that I hurried to get a closer look (I am susceptible to hallucinations at anything more than 50 metres!). It wasn't a jersey at all but a packet of biscuits and other groceries being clutched by an unsuspecting shopper. In a state of near ecstacy, I rushed back to my shop and designed my own tiger jersey.

I hope this serves to show that ideas are lurking everywhere, and those that stem from errors and brief glimpses are as wonderful (or better, according to Ms Takes, my lifelong tutor) than those over which we sweat tears.

DESIGN

CONTINUUM OF PERSONAL

- CRAFT ONLY
- NO PERSONAL DECISIONS
- EXTERNALLY IMPOSED RESTRAINTS

° Following a pattern to the letter, including the colours shown on the model.

° Using a pattern but changing the colours.

° Using a pattern but changing the stitch numbers or shape.

° Cutting out a jersey shape and laying it over a painting or picture and interpreting it in yarn.

° Random knitting within a limited colour range. Decision-making on the needles.

CONTENT IN DESIGN

CRAFT AND ART •
NUMEROUS PERSONAL DECISIONS •
SELF-IMPOSED RESTRAINTS •

° Cutting out coloured papers and laying these down in a pleasing design, possibly using self-imposed restraints.

° Designing on a blank page from a concept or object, with an awareness of line texture and colour and the human form.

° Combinations.

° Personal decisions on yarn, colours, concept, stitch types, garment silhouette, construction and embellishments.

FOLLOWING A PATTERN

Following a pattern to the letter, including using the colours specified, is a common enough activity — but even that requires a high level of skill. If you do decide to take this approach (yes, even unique knitters have been known to succumb), take full advantage of all the help and advice offered in the pattern. The information provided on the yarn ball band and in commercial patterns is explained further in Chapters 3 and 4, Yarns, and Measuring and mechanics.

Following a pattern exactly is usually a relaxing and satisfying activity, but there are disadvantages in this approach to knitting, and they're probably what brought this book to your attention in the first place. If you can knit that exact design, so can hundreds of other people. The satisfaction to be found in designing your own unique garment somewhat outshines that to be had by following a pattern. Probably you have followed many a pattern in your day and you're now ready for something new. Read on.

Using a pattern but changing the colours Using a pattern as a jumping-off point can provide a gentle introduction to designing a unique garment. By changing the colours but using the type of yarn specified, you can produce a more personal garment without the suspense of starting from a blank page. If you intend changing the colours in a commercial pattern, the following exercise may be useful.

Analyse the colour combinations used on the model and ask yourself the following questions:
° How many colours are used?
° Is there a main colour?
° Are the highlights lighter or darker (or both) than the main colour?
° Are the colours tonally matched?

This exercise is especially helpful when working from a picture in a magazine rather than a commercial pattern.

The next step is to do some quick sketches of the new colour scheme you are proposing. If drawing is not your favourite subject, trace several copies of the outline of the picture you are working off and try your colour schemes on the garment shapes you have traced. If the garment happens to be one you have seen on television, this could be just a tiny bit difficult, but it is not necessarily a problem. The garment you come up with may well be more interesting than the one you glimpsed, and you won't offend anyone by turning up at the same Hollywood party in an identical outfit!

Another method of obtaining a basic drawing to work on if your figure drawings look like kindergarten throwaways, is to trace figures from newspapers and magazines in different positions and with different silhouettes. (Generally, figure drawings in clothing magazines are elongated to improve the appearance of the garment being modelled. If this worries you, there are figure drawing books available and now would be a nice time to learn.)

Another alternative is to use photographs of yourself taken in simple poses and with minimal clothing. These can be glued to cardboard and cut out and traced. They make designs which suit your figure type easier to spot. (My only advice in this instance is that both photographer and photographee should swap places to avoid smugness on the part of the photographer!)

Using a pattern but changing the stitch numbers or shape To add width or length to a garment you need a little mathematical genius. Chapter 4, Measuring and mechanics includes instructions on how to work out a formula after knitting a sample swatch. Changing the basic shape of a garment may be as simple as adding extra stitches onto the width or as complex as changing a raglan sleeve to a batwing sleeve knitted on its side. In most cases, a sample swatch and tape measure are necessary evils for working out an altered garment size or shape.

THE OVERLAY DESIGN METHOD

This requires a degree of decision making. Choose a painting, picture, piece of carpet, whatever, then take a piece of paper or thin card and cut out of it a hole in the shape of a garment you like. Try a variety of silhouettes, sleeve shapes, necklines and sizes.

Place the paper or card on the painting or design and move the position of the cut-out hole until you see an idea you would like to knit.

This technique helps train the eye to see potential jerseys everywhere. By focusing on a small, restricted area, the mass of colour and line in a picture or design becomes less confusing and an object may be reduced to an obvious series of lines and blocks of colour. If further simplification is necessary before your "design" becomes knittable, try copying what you can see inside the cut-out shape onto another piece of paper. This will force you to make decisions, like whether a particular area is actually blue or red or contains flecks of both colours.

DESIGN

The accompanying series of photographs shows:

1. An original collage by Rosemary Mortimer (a New Zealand artist).
2. Several different-sized cut-outs giving different views of the collage.
3. A number of yarns blended into combinations which show some of the characteristics of the fabric they are intended to represent (in this case, hand-dyed silk and the plain selvedge edge of the collage). The approximate quantities of yarn required are also shown, by the bar graph form.
4. The finished jersey (with a V-neck instead of a round neck as in the original cut-out shape).

The change in medium from the original collage to the yarns used in the garment is an essential part of this design technique. Focusing on part of another artist's work and interpreting it in a new form is a complement and a tribute. Being eclectic is a natural prelude to artistic development.

USING THE GARMENT AS A CANVAS

A variation on the overlay method used on the previous page is to regard the garment as the picture canvas and

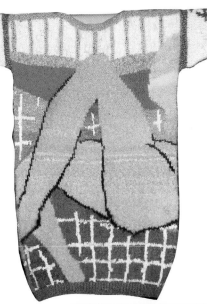

Left: Front of Matisse painting *Pink Nude* knitted as a dress by Lee Andersen. **Top Right:** Back of *Pink Nude*. **Right:** Klee Face by Heather Paterson.

"paint" on it with yarn an entire picture or design. Pictorial scenes from calendars or, better still, photographs from your own album are wonderful jumping-off points, providing designs employing colour, line and often opportunities for embroidery. The paintings of children and adults alike can lend themselves to interpretation in knitting.

In the accompanying photograph, Matisse's *Pink Nude,* painted in 1935, has been reproduced as a dress. The design is complete with the artist's signature, the title and date of the painting, all of which are knitted into the garment.

Above: A knitted ballerina based on a screen print by Pippa Sanderson. **Right:** Pippa's tryouts done when choosing a colour range for the screen print.   TC

DESIGN

DESIGNING FROM A CUT-OUT SILHOUETTE

The garment silhouette may be dictated by the wearer's body shape or by the lines already present in a painting or design being used as inspiration. If diagonals dominate the picture, a V-neck or boat neckline may work best. Curves within the design may suggest a crew or wide round neck. If you are using a Mondrian painting as a basis for your design, it may be best to incorporate square sleeves and a square neck, to reflect the geometric emphasis of the lines in the painting. Of course, you always have the option of deliberately incorporating a round neck in a generally square design for contrast.

Necks and sleeves each have one main function. The neck opening is there to let the head through the garment and to ensure that the garment remains on the shoulders. Sleeves, if present, are generally intended to keep the arms warm and are not meant to dangle in the crayfish mornay!

A good healthy attitude to design involves constantly asking, "Why not?" There may be practical reasons for rejecting some ideas, but often the reason they haven't been done before is that no one has tried them.

A good exercise for budding designers is to draw quick sketches of every type of neckline that you know of, then try to think of three more. Do the same for sleeve lines and bottom lines and general garment construction (that is, the shapes of the pieces and how they fit together). Some ideas are illustrated here.

Choose a silhouette to suit your shape. After drawing the outline, possibilities emerge for echoing the garment lines in the body of the knitting. A crew neck and leg of mutton sleeves may suggest further curves and cables within the body. A deep V-neck may suggest diagonals and Mondrian-type divisions. A batwing garment with its wide triangular canvas may suggest zig-zags emanating from a central point.

NECKLINES IN DESIGN

Necklines are an important part of good design because they form the border between the garment and the face. The neckline needs to belong and complement both.

You may devise brand-new, never-been-seen-before necklines by focusing on one of the design elements from within the garment when designing the neckline. Practical considerations may affect the

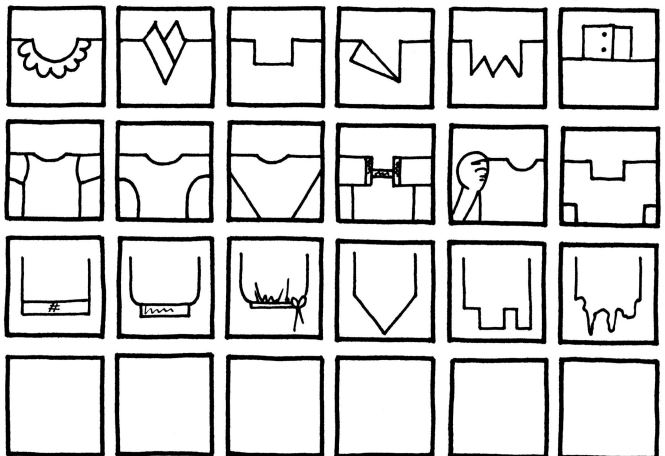

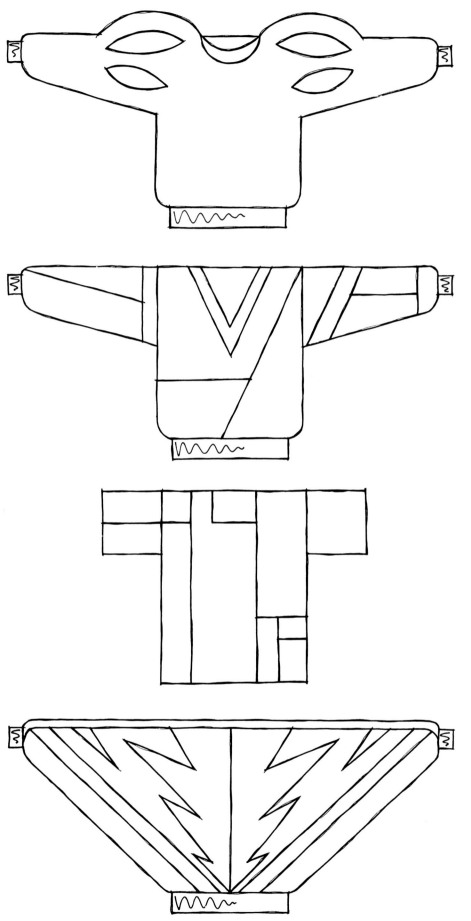

choice of design. If the garment is very heavy and warm, a warm neckline (or at least one that can be altered to provide warmth when it is cold) is probably sensible. Delicate evening designs may suggest deep, cutaway backs or off-the-shoulder, strappy necklines.

RANDOM KNITTING

Tactile fibres and random stitch patterns and colour blocks can be combined into interesting garments. However, different weights of yarns within a single garment can provide traps for new players. Suggestions on how to deal with these may be found in Chapter 4, Measuring and mechanics.

A monochromatic or single colour scheme may be an effective foil to the chaos created by random changes of texture and stitch patterns within a garment. White, cream, ecru, black or grey are often used effectively in such "experiments". There is, of course, no reason why such a garment shouldn't be knitted in bright red or lots of bold, bright colours. The deciding factor will be what *you* want to *wear* or indeed what *you enjoy* knitting.

PIN THE TAIL ON THE GARMENT

This method of designing is one of the simplest. Even a child can do it — in fact, probably the best idea is to ask a child to do just that.

The basic outline of the garment is drawn on a piece of paper. Pick out the required colours, then shut your eyes and draw, scribble, dot and wiggle the pencils or crayons without trying to keep within the outline. The result, when knitted and confined within the garment shape, will be a free, dramatic design.

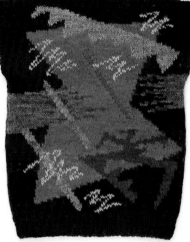

TC

Above: Kate Wells, who designed and knitted, spun and dyed this garment, does not actually design with cut paper. She does, however, have an awareness of layered images providing depth and interest to a design.

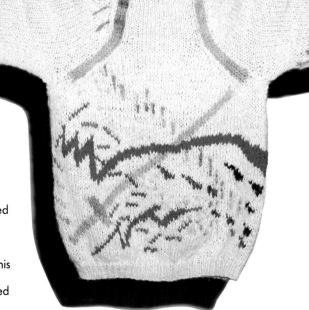

Top: Mocha, a random knit designed and knitted by Mary Hazlewood.
Centre: A zig zag necked batwing.
Right: The centre section of a scribble pad supplied the idea for this design incorporating random dip-dyed yarns. Designed and knitted by Lee Andersen.

THE CUT-AND-STICK METHOD

In this method small pieces of appropriately coloured paper are cut into shapes and assembled into pleasing designs. The paper may be shaped into circles or squares, for example. As part of the game you may even impose limitations, such as using *every* scrap in the design. This means that the negative shapes or leftovers are as important as the initial shapes that were cut out.

An advantage of this design method is the layering effect which remains apparent in the finished garment. A simple concept can result in a complex and sophisticated design.

THE COLD-TURKEY METHOD

A complex design may originate from examining a single object, including its colours, lines and silhouette. The object chosen may provide

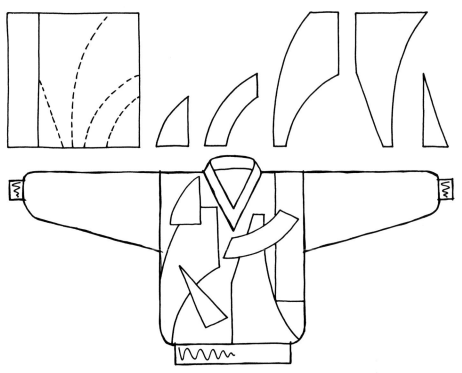

ideas for incorporating unusual yarns and fibres in a garment and, perhaps, embroidery and beading techniques.

The batwing (actually butterfly wing!) garment photographed is based on the underside of the male yellow admiral butterfly of Australia. The body is interpreted in handspun St Bernard dog hair, and the white edges and blue spots are embroidered onto the knitting.

Petra McCorquodale interpreted a yellow admiral butterfly in knitting.   TC

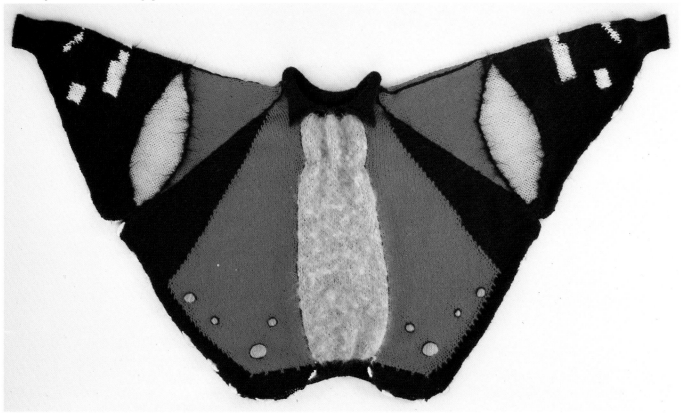

FINDING IDEAS

From the environment This can be done anywhere: at the zoo, or at the library with pad and coloured pencils in hand; while you're in the shower, going for a walk or just relaxing. When you're in the kitchen, working or relaxing in the garden or at the beach, look carefully at what's around you. A shell, the stove, a single leaf or the vague impression of a remembered garden may provide wonderful ideas.

Your own paintings, children's work, prints and paintings in galleries and books; pots (ceramics and kitchen implements); all are likely design sources. Look at all things with an eye for *colour,* then with *line* in mind, then again, thinking of *outline* shapes. Don't be afraid of being eclectic; ideas that stem from other people's ideas are fine. Just make sure you acknowledge the source if you can and return the borrowed idea by making something that can give ideas to others. As many of us are aware, it is a very long way from an idea to a wearable garment and a lot can happen in the process.

In-depth study of a single idea
Frequently, one jersey in the making will inspire the idea for the next garment. A set of black and white stripes alone could offer infinite design ideas. It may even be necessary to limit the inspiration further to black and and white lines of the same width, with no wiggles. Tightening the rules can force lateral thinking, which is always good for the brain. Get into the habit of drawing at least five versions of an idea. Drawing speeds up the process of designing, making it unnecessary to knit up every idea to see how well it works. Lots of drawing eases the need to make each jersey the ultimate garment.

Ultimate jerseys tend to be so ominously important that they are never begun! Or they are begun but are constantly unpulled or hidden away in frustration . . . like a child that turned out to be a person instead of what the parent had in mind. The idea in your head, the garment in your mind's eye, is just that! What happens on the needles is something else again.

Sometimes it may be necessary to put away a half-finished garment for a while (watch the moths though), to be pulled out and looked at afresh later. Try tipping the garment upside

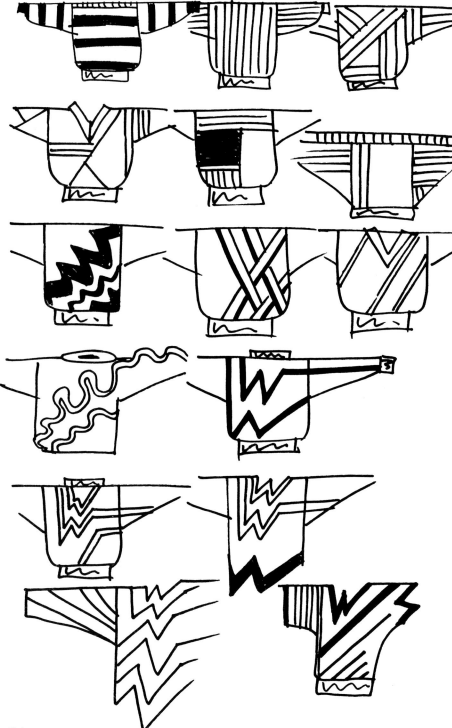

down, turning it inside out, cutting it up or sewing on bits (read the chapter on disasters). But most of all, learn from it. No effort is wasted. Discover at least one new thing every time you knit!

Metamorphosis Contrast and movement are the two elements a hunter uses to spot the prey. Just as they are essential to the hunt, these concepts can be key factors in effective design. Any design involving more than one colour, type of line, stitch pattern or shape has contrast. The design can be static (for example, various different-coloured blocks arranged in a formal manner), but if movement is introduced the garment will be more visually exciting. Movement leads the eye through the design, taking the observer on a journey through the garment.

Transitions from dark to light areas, from active line to passive line and even from fat rectangles to thin rectangles are movements between extremes. Such movement and change, or evolution from one design element to another, can be called metamorphosis. Metamorphosis can occur in a single direction, or it may take place simultaneously in two directions. A design may

include a central rod that develops in one direction into a spot or circle and into a triangle in the other direction. Crosses may even *cross* a gentle transition from one colour to another. Use your imagination to devise such visual puns.

Word games A design idea may surface in a conversation with a joke, or even with a single unusual word.

Words and even single letters are designs in their own right. When reduced to a series of lines and shapes, many of them are interesting and ask for attention because by their very nature they suggest communication. They are trying to tell us something.

Words and letters have been used extremely effectively by Ruby Brilliant, an Australian designer, who has based many of her works on Vincent's Pain Relief tins. The words on the tins, and even the price, are incorporated in her garments.

THREE-DIMENSIONAL HUMAN FORM

Because its surfaces are curved, a garment to be worn and moved about in is even more exciting to design upon than the flat surface used by most graphic artists. Lines on a garment distort and alter during movement, creating further interaction and interest.

On a flat surface a diagonal line is just that — diagonal and straight. However, the same diagonal when placed on a sewn-up sleeve on the human form becomes a curve. If you plan it well, several diagonal lines can be placed on a sleeve and joined at the seam to produce a spiral. In this case, each succeeding diagonal line must begin on the opposite edge and in the same row as the end of the previous one. Because of the very nature of knitting, with its row-by-row construction, such planning is relatively logical and simple.

A further area to be explored is the interaction of colour caused by movement of the human form. Let's use a simple example — a jersey with a blue body, one orange sleeve and one yellow sleeve. When modelled with the wearer standing straight with arms at the sides, the sleeves would provide a contrasting frame to the body, and each would subtly alter the appearance of the blue alongside the sleeve. If the

arms were folded, the whole would become a blend of yellow and orange or harmonious (analogous) colours, bordered by contrasting (complementary) blue.

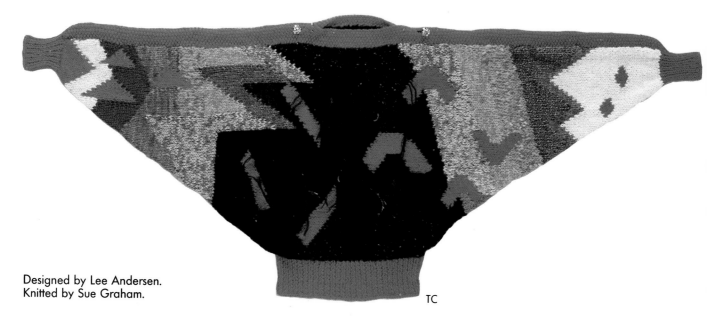

Designed by Lee Andersen.
Knitted by Sue Graham.

TC

COMBINED DESIGN TECHNIQUES

Several or all of the foregoing design techniques may be combined for a single project, leading to a design that is uniquely your own. Naturally the most personal garments result from individual decisionmaking at all stages. If every aspect, every variable, shows thought and integrity towards a chosen design concept, the result will be very special.

The technical skills used in the execution of such "works

of art" are also essential ingredients. Without these skills and a knowledge of the fibres and how to use them, frustration and disappointment are more likely to occur.

Art and craft, head and hand, working together are an unbeatable and enviable combination. They can be yours.

For further practical information on design techniques see the following sections: Using a cartoon (Chapter 6 Intarsia); Fairisle graphs and charts, Designing your own Fairisle (Chapter 5).

Above: Arrows combining fabric and knitting. **Below left:** Metropolis with embroidered graffiti. **Above left and Below:** Lee Andersen's interpretation of a garden by a left-handed artist.

TC

ACTIVE AND PASSIVE LINES

Like colours, lines cannot help but stimulate a response, conscious or otherwise. Just as red is an action colour, diagonal lines are decisive action lines.

Complementary colours such as yellow and purple create excitement. Short lines apparently moving in many directions also give a feeling of excitement and even disorientation.

Blues and mid-greys can engender a sense of calm and inertia; so, too, can horizontal lines. This feeling is further accentuated if the horizontal lines are also indecisive at the edges, trailing off as if they have run out of steam.

A characteristic of horizontal lines which is often ignored, to the detriment of appearances, is their tendency to lead the eye outwards, making the area they span appear wider than it actually is. Admittedly, horizontal lines are the easiest to knit, but I believe this very fact was the result of a malicious act on the part of diet-formula manufacturers during the year dot!

Vertical lines lead the eye up and down, making the area they span appear taller and thinner. Feelings of strength and honour may be associated

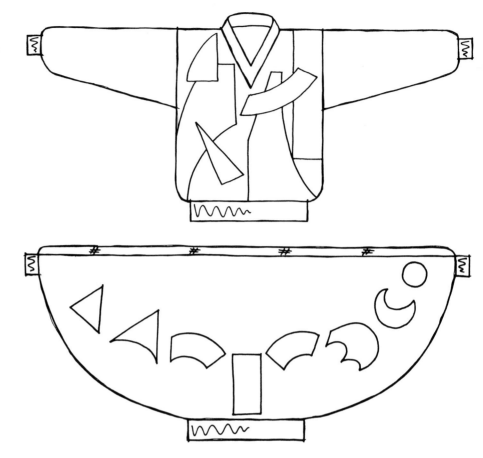

with vertical lines. Diagonals can also provide strength if they tend towards the upright state.

ACTIVE AND PASSIVE SHAPES

Geometric shapes are universal, precise and contained. When they are altered (for instance, a square into a loose rhomboid) they suggest speed and movement. Appropriately, speed and

movement is precisely what is required to draw them in this way.

SYMBOLS

When drawing out a design I find it helpful to use symbols for the various stitch patterns I wish to use. Those I have found useful are illustrated in the accompanying drawing. You may wish to develop your own as your favourite stitches become apparent.

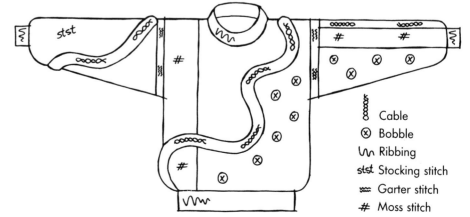

Cable
Bobble
Ribbing
stst Stocking stitch
Garter stitch
Moss stitch

TRADITIONAL KNITTING

Icelandic knitting

Fair Isle knitting

Aran knitting

Norwegian knitting

Alpaca knitting from Peru

Guernsey

Jersey

Irish crochet

Argyle vest

Shetland lace

Aaron Piper, aged 11, in the jersey he designed for himself.   TC
Knitted by Sandra Green.

Chanel Taewhaki, aged 9, in the jersey she designed.
Knitted by Sandra Green.

Michael Watt, 10 years, designed this toddler's jacket, knitted by Jean Rees.

CHAPTER THREE

YARNS

Anything flexible can be knitted. Fine wire can be knitted, videotape can be knitted, even the shorn coat of a sheep can be knitted. But before choosing the right material or combinations of materials, decisions need to be made regarding the intended use of the product and the object of the exercise.

If your intention is to make exquisite knitted jewellery, the best materials may be combinations of fine silver wire and perhaps dyed silk thread. Damaged videotapes or full feature film tapes would make an appropriate noise-making, reflective and flexible knitted backdrop for a theatre production. Clothing, by definition, has to have certain characteristics which may dictate the choice of fibres, but these are not as restrictive as you may have thought.

Clothing generally covers part or all of the human form. It may be designed to protect, warm, decorate or hide parts of the anatomy. Most often, it is required to be removable without damaging the person or the article. It should probably be washable or cleanable, also without damage. For comfort and practicality, it is usually flexible or includes flexible components at appropriate places — that is, elbows, knees and armholes.

The product of knitting is always a flexible fabric — an ideal medium for covering and/or decorating the human body. Knitted fabric for clothing can be made from many different individual fibres or combinations of fibres. The characteristics of the most commonly used fibres in knitting are listed in the following charts.

TYPES OF YARN

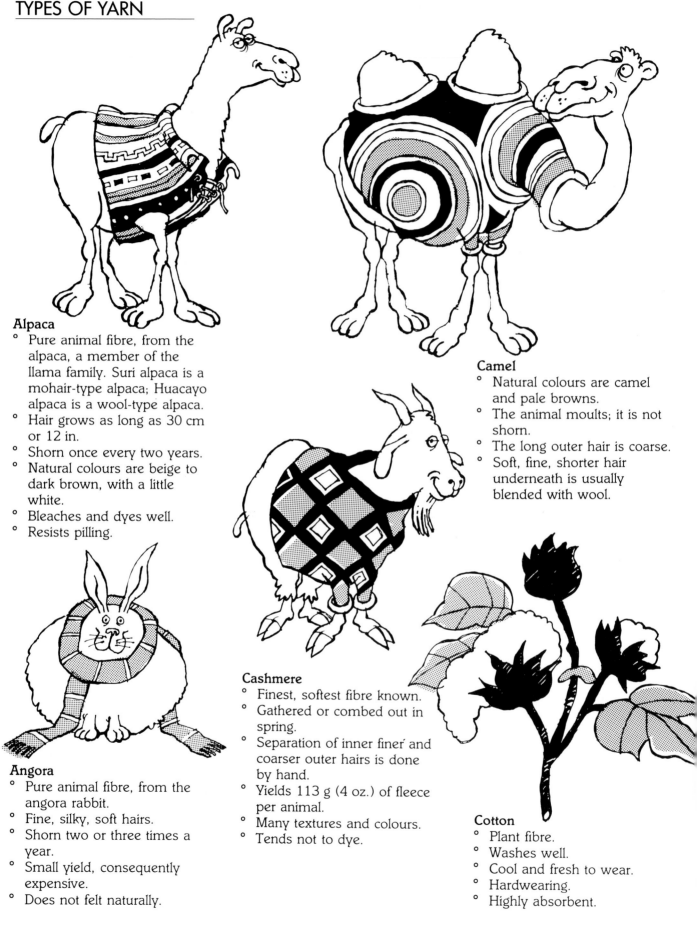

Alpaca
° Pure animal fibre, from the alpaca, a member of the llama family. Suri alpaca is a mohair-type alpaca; Huacayo alpaca is a wool-type alpaca.
° Hair grows as long as 30 cm or 12 in.
° Shorn once every two years.
° Natural colours are beige to dark brown, with a little white.
° Bleaches and dyes well.
° Resists pilling.

Camel
° Natural colours are camel and pale browns.
° The animal moults; it is not shorn.
° The long outer hair is coarse.
° Soft, fine, shorter hair underneath is usually blended with wool.

Angora
° Pure animal fibre, from the angora rabbit.
° Fine, silky, soft hairs.
° Shorn two or three times a year.
° Small yield, consequently expensive.
° Does not felt naturally.

Cashmere
° Finest, softest fibre known.
° Gathered or combed out in spring.
° Separation of inner finer and coarser outer hairs is done by hand.
° Yields 113 g (4 oz.) of fleece per animal.
° Many textures and colours.
° Tends not to dye.

Cotton
° Plant fibre.
° Washes well.
° Cool and fresh to wear.
° Hardwearing.
° Highly absorbent.

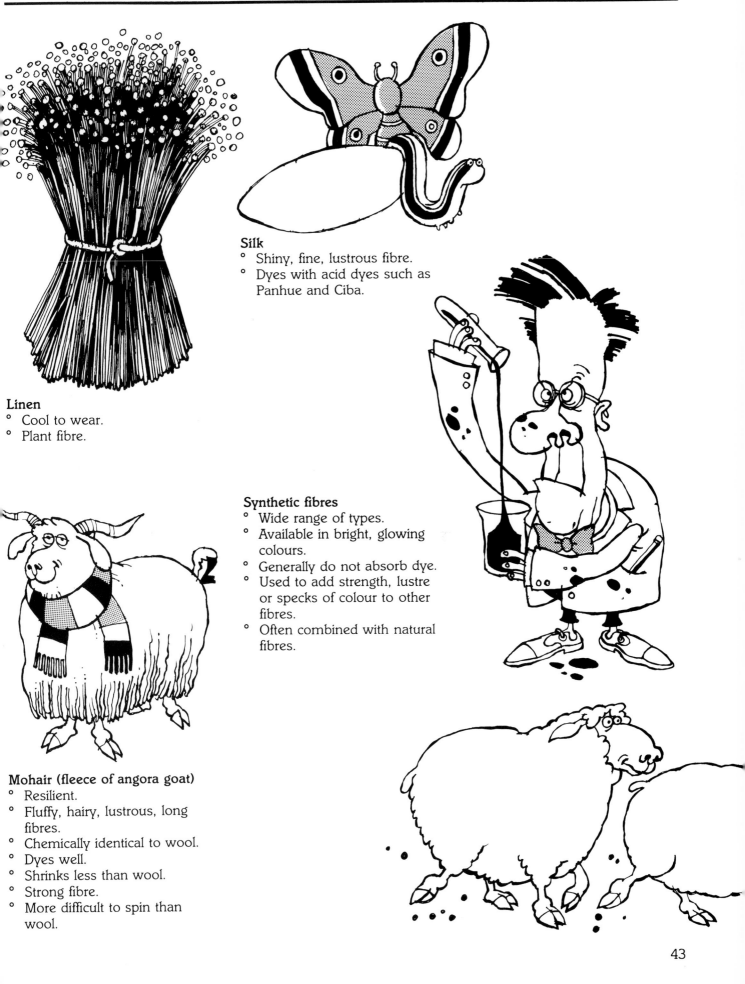

Silk
- Shiny, fine, lustrous fibre.
- Dyes with acid dyes such as Panhue and Ciba.

Linen
- Cool to wear.
- Plant fibre.

Synthetic fibres
- Wide range of types.
- Available in bright, glowing colours.
- Generally do not absorb dye.
- Used to add strength, lustre or specks of colour to other fibres.
- Often combined with natural fibres.

Mohair (fleece of angora goat)
- Resilient.
- Fluffy, hairy, lustrous, long fibres.
- Chemically identical to wool.
- Dyes well.
- Shrinks less than wool.
- Strong fibre.
- More difficult to spin than wool.

70 MILLION SHEEP CAN'T BE WRONG!

They know that nothing has the look and feel of 100 per cent pure new wool. And with all the colours and styles available in Woolmark yarns, it's not hard to imagine yourself in your own "designer knit" at any time of the year. Wool may just be the best thing to happen to your wardrobe! Here's why wool is my favourite fibre.

Wool
- Pure animal fibre, only available from sheep.
- Natural colours are creamy white, silver, brownish, grey, charcoal.
- Dyes well with good depth of colour and good colour retention.
- Absorbs up to 30 per cent of its own weight in moisture. Absorbs moisture from the body, making the wearer more comfortable. Absorbs moisture from the air in a process that creates heat.
- Crease resistant (has natural crimp — waviness).
- Supple, easy to work with, glides over the needles.
- Easily compacted.
- Strong and durable when properly cared for (woollen garments have been known

to survive for more than 2,000 years).
- Stretches and recovers well, is naturally elastic, holds its shape because of its natural crimp.
- Keeps its good looks longer.
- Naturally oil resistant. Has a low degree of static elasticity and doesn't attract dirt.
- Cool in summer, warm in winter.
- Repels water. Can ward off a light shower.
- The crimp of wool traps air when fibres are spun together, providing insulation. Light in weight for bulk.
- Hand washable and dry cleanable. Can be made machine washable.
- Lambswool is from the first shear. It has one rounded tip.
- Wool can be boiled without spoiling if heat is raised slowly from a low temperature.
- It can be made to felt (Ms Takes frequently felts knitted garments during washing).
- Naturally flame resistant, self extinguishing and burns slowly, even when in contact with an open flame.
- Pills when rubbed extensively, depending on the amount of twist in the yarn.

EVERYTHING YOU ALWAYS WANTED TO KNOW ABOUT SHEEP

The first sheep in New Zealand were landed by Captain James Cook on one of his voyages. These two merinos died soon afterwards but it was the beginning of New Zealand's sheep industry. Whalers probably brought others, but the first flock of any size was 100 merinos owned by a Mr Wright, on Mana Island near Wellington, in 1834.

Many of the early sheepfarmers were well-to-do Englishmen who came to New Zealand to found new estates. Land was cheap at this time, but sheep were expensive. Men and women roughed it while clearing the bush to create pasture land. By the 1840s thousands of sheep arrived from the large stations in Australia. By 1885 there were 763,000 sheep in New Zealand and nine years later, nearly five million.

Merinos are now only a small part of the national flock, with many breeds developed specifically for New Zealand's climate.

Today there are over 73 million sheep providing just over 45 per cent of the world's coarse wool. New Zealand is second only to Australia in wool production for international use and has a domestic per capita wool consumption that is the second highest in the world after Iceland.

But it is not only all of those sheep on the hills of New Zealand that have convinced Kiwis that wool is a good thing. In a climate that is temperate, yet can experience extremes of temperature and many weather variations in a single afternoon, wool is the perfect working fibre.

The wool on a sheep's back grows in tufts called "staples". All these staples are kinked from end to end in waves of even curls ∿∿. The finer the wool, the tighter this curl, which is called "crimp". Every strand of wool carries its own crimp forever.

In a wool garment, this crimp helps make the fibres stand apart from each other and traps little pockets of air between the fibres just like water is trapped in a sponge. Still air is one of the best insulators in Nature.

If you looked at a single wool fibre under a microscope, it would look like a palm tree. There is a very fine membrane covering the scales of the fibre which keeps liquid out of the fibre's core — almost like a mini-raincoat. The membrane is so thin that water-vapour can pass through it to the inside of the fibre.

Because of this unique breathability, wool keeps you warmer in winter and cooler in summer. In a rainy winter climate, wool jerseys keep out the cold and stay warmer longer, even if they get wet.

Wool just simply can't absorb water like other fibres — just try mopping up spilt water with a wool cloth!

Wool attracts the water-vapour your body produces when you get hot and steamy and passes it on to the outside air. The Bedouin Arabs always wear loose wool garments to protect them from the fierce desert sun. And New Zealand shearers wear wool singlets no matter what the weather because they are more comfortable and stand up to the abuse of hard work.

Wool really is Nature's miracle fibre. And it is tested for comfort by the original owner even before it gets to you in the form of handknitting yarns, wool suits, coats or blankets.

IT'S ALL RELATIVE

New Zealand has so many sheep that I just can't resist a few crazy statistics. If you take *all* the animals in New Zealand people would be outnumbered 28 to 1! In fact, the relationship of sheep to people (a pretty good one, really) is exactly opposite in Japan. Our illustrations make the point with a bit of tongue in cheek . . .

Pure New Wool

The Woolmark is the world's best known textile symbol. The Woolmark is the customer's assurance that the product is 100 per cent pure new wool *and* that it has met strict quality standards in its manufacture.

Created for the International Wool Secretariat, the Woolmark today is recognised by over 400 million people in over 50 countries. Worldwide, some 15,500 companies (over 300 in New Zealand) are licensed to use the Woolmark in association with their products. More than 300 million Woolmark labels are used each month on products ranging from carpets to textiles to handknitting yarns and all sorts of apparel.

When you buy Woolmark yarns, you can be sure that they have been thoroughly tested for strength, colour fastness, and quality. So when you knit your masterpiece, it will be as beautiful in years to come as it is today. Look for the Woolmark quality symbol on your handknitting yarns.

APPEARANCE VERSUS COMFORT

In some types of clothing the decorative element may have higher priority than comfort. A summer dress that will be worn frequently must be both decorative and feel nice against the skin as well as hide those socially defined private areas. A winter coat may be decorative and protect against the cold, but the way it feels against the skin will probably be assigned a low priority.

Different people have different responses to various fibres. Most love wool and mohair; others may feel the same way about these fibres but be unable to wear them in certain forms against sensitive areas, such as the neck and wrists. A particular blend, spinning technique and quality of fibre may be necessary to overcome this. If an allergy to a fibre that you admire is destroying your love of life and furry things, try lining the finished garment with stretch fabric or design your garments to include only small amounts of the problem fibre, surrounded by one you can wear comfortably.

Fibres do often become softer after washing with a wool cleanser such as Softly. Alternatively, glycerine added to the washing water can soften a hard fibre.

PLYS

The term "ply" is used, sometimes indiscriminately, to the confusion of us all. A homespinner generally spins two "plys" or threads. When these are twisted together (referred to as plying) into a single yarn, the thread is strengthened. A "Z" twist single thread is spun with the wheel turning to the right. An "S" twist single is spun with the spinning wheel turning to the left.

Yarns that have too much twist at the plying stage of the process make the knitted stitches slope to the left. Yarns with insufficient twist in the plying make the knitted stitches slope to the right.

Plying decreases the risk of warping in the finished garment. When a thread is spun, it is twisted in a certain direction. By plying together two or more threads, the twist is neutralised. According to this use of the term "ply", three separate threads or plys twisted together form a 3 ply yarn. If four are plied together, a 4 ply yarn is made. The plys are equal in thickness in classic handknitting yarns.

Commercial spinners and yarn manufacturers define the term "ply" differently. When a commercial yarn is labelled 2 ply it is not necessarily made up of two plys or threads twisted together. In commercial terminology, a 2 ply yarn is thin, and the length of the yarn in a 50 g ball is equal to that of all other 2 ply 50 g balls.

The "ply" referred to on the ball band is a quick guide to the gauge of the yarn. If you have chosen a 16 ply, pink, 100 per cent wool yarn and wish to use a similar gauge grey mohair yarn from another manufacturer, look first for one that is designated 16 ply (assuming you do not wish to change stitch numbers or needle sizes when changing yarn).

NOVELTY YARNS

Although most novelty yarns are made up of two strands twisted together, they may not have a stated ply. The ball band may carry a diagram of a 10 × 10 cm (4 × 4 in.) swatch, including stitch numbers to obtain the gauge shown. Most novelty yarns may be knitted on small needles to form a solid-textured fabric; alternatively, very large needles may be used with equal success for an interesting bobbly, holey look.

Novelty yarns may be manufactured or handspun by plying a single tight thread with a very loose and perhaps lumpy one. Such yarns are referred to as bouclés (pronounced boo-clays). A thick, loosely twisted yarn may be strengthened by wrapping it or running it with a fine, perhaps synthetic, thread.

Lurex or glitter threads have been known to tarnish and the glitter wear off. This should not be a problem if you buy a lurex yarn with a polyester base for knitting clothing.

CHOOSING A SUITABLE YARN WEIGHT

Depending on the purpose of your planned creation, certain fibres and thicknesses of yarns will be more appropriate than others. You would not use an 18 ply, thick, lumpy, dog-hair yarn if you wanted to knit a shawl that could be pulled through a wedding ring. Fine merino lambswool would be more appropriate. Similarly, you wouldn't choose a fine merino 2 ply and 6 mm needles if you were planning to wear the garment while sliding down a mountainside. Beyond such obvious limitations, use your own initiative in deciding which weight of yarn to use.

It is not necessary to work with a single yarn type or thickness in one garment. It can be exciting to work with great changes in texture, combinations of fine yarns, thick fluffy ones and even strips of fabric and bits of string.

HOW MUCH YARN DO I NEED?

The answer to this question is preferably as much as you can buy, carry home and store or as much as you can shear off a passing sheep. (Here in New Zealand sheep walk down the street, dot the hillsides and cover our car seats.) Knitters of unique garments are frequently inspired to begin a new project at any time of the day or night. A wardrobe or, better, room full of yarn is a wonderful asset to such a person. Whether you have such a treasure chest or buy your yarn for each garment, you'll need to know how to work out the quantities required.

Deciding how much yarn you need for a garment is, in fact, relatively simple. Weigh a garment, coat, scarf or jersey, that is of approximately the same size and weight as you envisage your creation and use that as a guide. If you can find nothing like what you have in mind, check pattern books for a comparable garment.

For a long-sleeved, hip-length garment in relatively fine yarn you will require about 300 g (11 oz.); in double knitting yarn you will need around 500 g (18 oz.); in chunky yarn you'll need about 700 g (25 oz.). Huge, sloppy garments in super-thick yarn may weigh more than a kilo, or 1,000 g (35 oz.).

If you are planning a very formal garment in which the influence of Ms Takes will not be welcome, it is probably best to work out fairly precisely the amount of yarn required so you can buy it all from the same dye lot. Dye lots can vary in tone quite markedly, sufficient to make an obvious line if the changeover takes place in the middle of a sleeve. A complete sleeve in a different dye lot from the main part of the garment, however, is not as noticeable.

The most accurate way to determine the required amount of yarn of a particular type is to knit up a ball in a medium colour in the chosen stitch pattern. (Darker colours tend to contain more dyestuff, which can effect the thickness of the yarn.) The knittable area from a particular ball depends also on the fibre content of the yarn, its texture, thickness and weight, the amount of twist present and, of course, the tension and stitch pattern. The following guidelines generally apply:

° Synthetics go further than wool.
° Fluffy, finer yarns go further than thicker, heavier yarns.
° Yarns with a loose twist go further than those with tighter twist.
° A loose tension causes less yarn to be used.
° Tight cabled and built-up stitch patterns use more yarn.

Once you've knitted up the ball, measure the size of the swatch, then work out the total surface area of the garment. Divide the total surface area by the area of the swatch to find the number of balls of yarn required.

If you begin a new ball at the beginning of the main body of a garment, directly above the ribbing at the bottom edge, the area knitted by the end of the ball will also provide a good guide to the number of balls required for the remainder of the garment. (Ribbing uses more yarn in relation to area than plain knitting.)

Information on yarn weight and length is listed in both metrics and imperials on many yarn bands, but at times you may need to convert quantities. Remember that 28 g equals approximately 1 oz.

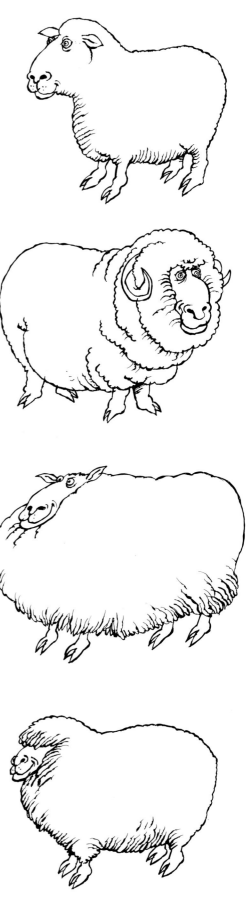

BLENDING OF YARNS FOR THICKNESS

It is possible, but not advisable for large areas of knitting, to separate plys to make a thicker yarn into a thinner ply. This can be done by splitting or cutting and pulling out one or more threads or plys. It has the effect of unbalancing the twist and weakening the yarn, but if you acknowledge this (and perhaps run a cotton thread with the weakened yarn) it can be used successfully. Some single-ply yarns are made commercially.

It is always easier to thicken

Blended yarn jersey, designed by Lee Andersen, knitted by Stephanie Wynne.

Handspun novelty yarns by Margery Rae.

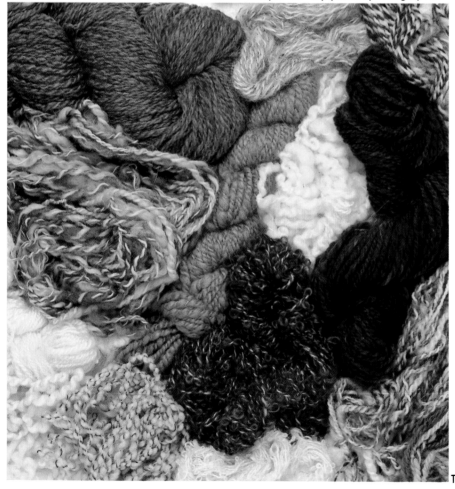

a yarn to match the thickest fibre in your work, by running two or more yarns together. A great advantage of combining yarns in this way is that you can blend several slightly different tones of one colour to give a depth of colour not otherwise attainable. Extreme differences among the combined yarns create a rich, flecked effect. By adding a textured yarn to a plain one you can create a yarn that is uniquely yours.

A further advantage of blending your own combinations of yarns is that you can "pull together" different colours within a garment, giving them a common element — that is, by twisting one yarn with every other yarn in the garment. For example, a fine blue yarn run with all the other yarns in the garment will create an harmonious effect.

Test the knitted thickness of such combinations by knitting sample swatches and measuring the gauge (see Chapter 4, Measuring and mechanics). If you wish to match a blended yarn to a bought yarn, try this quick test. Twist the combined yarn tightly, then twist the bought yarn. If they seem to be of matching thickness when twisted, they will tend to knit up similarly.

Wool winders are available from most shops dealing in knitting yarn accessories. These are especially valuable if you wish to combine two or more yarns ready for knitting as a single thread without plying them through a spinning wheel.

MAKING YOUR OWN YARNS

Spinning It is viable to handspin your own yarns, particularly novelty yarns, if you have access to a spinning wheel, a tutor and a tame sheep. The ability to spin means you will not only be able to use unique yarns not commercially available but you will have an instant use for all those combed and moulted hairs from the family dog.

Many books are available on handspinnable fibres and handspinning. For advice and information, contact one of the spinners and weavers guilds, present throughout the country.

Kiwicraft Kiwicraft is a process in which wool is knitted directly from the fleece without first spinning it into a yarn on a spinning wheel. It is slow but satisfying and fills in an evening if you happen to get stuck in a sheep paddock overnight without your trusty spinning wheel! (The technique was used in shearing sheds by Maori women, who used manuka twigs or no. 8 fencing wire as knitting needles.)

It involves knitting shorn fleece as it is or after it has been carded, or separated and straightened, in much the same way as cleaning and carding is used to prepare a fleece for handspinning. The twisting and plying that is normally done with the aid of a spinning wheel is eliminated. The fleece is knitted as a single ply, and sometimes the twist that occurs naturally in the knitting process is the only twist present in the yarn. The wool can be rolled or rubbed against the thigh before knitting to add more twist.

Commercial spinning or handspinning normally adds strength and durability to the yarn. Because this step is left

Balls of wound wool and a kiwicrafted, knitted man by Margery Rae. TC

out, Kiwicrafted work is not as strong as knitted spun yarn, but it makes a lovely, soft fabric, exhibits a skill and is most satisfying to perform.

MAKING FABRIC KNITTABLE

Fine fabric scraps can be made knittable by cutting them into strips along the bias of the material. (Bias cutting ensures some element of elasticity.) You can knot strips together and knit them that way for a fringed effect, or knit them together with a fine yarn for a textured but more restrained effect. Some fabrics will fray along the edges when cut, reminiscent of chenille.

Before attempting to knit fabric strips, test them with a gentle tug. If they pull apart, it will be necessary to cut them wider and knit them folded, or to run them together with a strong thread in case the twisting inherent in knitting does not provide sufficient strength.

A degree of strength is important if a garment including knitted strips is intended to last. If you are

concerned about strength, yet still wish to use a particular "weak" fabric, place the finished garment in a pantihose or stocking foot when washing and drying it. Tie off the foot to restrict any drag or movement during washing.

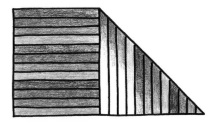

LOOKING AFTER WOOLLEN KNITS

Wool keeps you warm and toasty when you're out and about on chilly winter days. And when you come inside, wool's unique breathability means that your body can adjust quickly to room temperature. Wool is easy to clean and keeps its shape no matter how many times you wash it. And best of all, the durability of wool means that your favourite jersey will still be your favourite jersey for years to come.

Here's how to take care of your original:

Washing For best results, turn your jersey inside out. Fill a basin with lukewarm water (enough to cover the garment) and add a small amount of approved wool detergent such as Softly. Let soak for a few minutes, then gently press the water through the garment. *Do not* pull, twist or rub the jersey, as this may cause felting. Rinse three or four times in lukewarm water until water is clear. (Garments may also be drycleaned.)

Some yarns are machine washable. Check the label on the ball band and follow the care instructions.

Drying In the basin, press out excess water then roll in a thick towel to remove as much of the remaining water as possible. Dry flat on a towel away from direct sunlight and heat, whilst ensuring the garment is not stretched by excessive handling. If necessary, shape the garment on a soft, padded board and press through a clean, damp cloth. Press rather than iron the garment.

Storage Clean, shake and air the garment before putting it

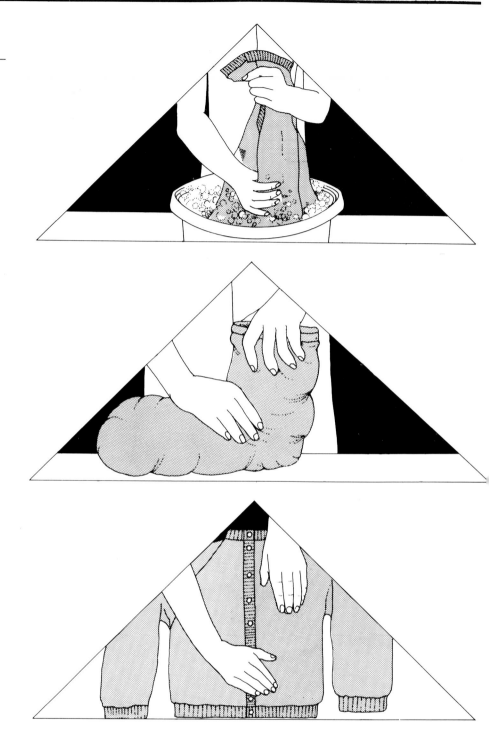

away to ensure longer life. Lay flat; do not hang. When jerseys are stored folded, do not store in a plastic bag as this does not allow wool to breathe.

Repairs Always keep a bit of wool used in making the garment for later repairs.

Attach a dolly of yarn to an inside seam and wash it with the garment. You will then have an exact match should a repair be necessary in the future. Repairs to informal garments need not be so carefully matched. See Disasters, Chapter 9.

Shirring or hat elastic can be threaded through ribbing for a tighter fit if the garment becomes loose after washing.

CHOOSING YARN BY PERSONALITY

It has been observed that yarn choosers seem to fall into four distinct categories:

Normal knitter type These people collect everything in the colour range they've decided upon. Then they design the garment and go and buy what they wanted but don't have . . . generally the main colours.

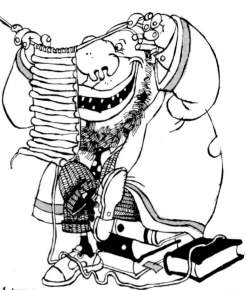

The judicial type
These people love a challenge. They use only the yarns in the house and they use *all* of those yarns in the garment.

The disgustingly self-disciplined shopper type
These people design their entire garment, then purchase all the yarns *exactly* as they first decided and bypass all eager little balls of fluff that would offer themselves for delight.

Fanatical hoarder type
Membership of Yarn Hoarders Anonymous is recommended, but there is no known cure. Yarn hoarders buy and hide under beds (even divans) all sorts of wonderful yarns, but they never use them because they are too beautiful.

MAKING A DOLLY

A yarn dolly is useful in Fairisle and intarsia knitting. It is pulled or unwound from the middle and keeps a small length of yarn tidy and unlikely to unroll itself.

The dolly illustrated is made as follows. Wind the yarn clockwise around your thumb several times to secure the end that will be used to start the knitting. Cross your palm with

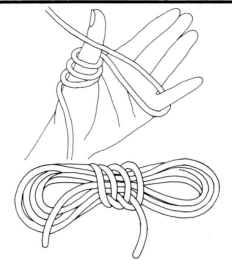

the yarn and take it around the outside of your little finger and back to your palm via the gap between your little finger and your ring finger. Carry the yarn around the outside of your thumb, clockwise, and take it back across your palm to the outside of your little finger. Repeat this figure-of-eight movement about 10 times. Tie off the yarn by making three half hitches around the middle of the dolly over your palm.

CHAPTER FOUR

MEASURING & MECHANICS

This chapter offers solutions to a range of questions that begin with 'how?' How many stitches do I cast on to make a garment fit me? How do I make a bobble?

It acknowledges the usefulness of commercial patterns, stitch pattern books, tape measures and pins.

Essentially it recommends that the original knitter in their enthusiasm does not throw the baby out with the bath water.

USING COMMERCIAL PATTERNS

In a commercial pattern, basic stitch numbers, stitch gauge or tension and needle sizes are given at the beginning. It is advisable to check your tension against that stated in the pattern, unless you belong to Ms Takes school of thought; she particularly likes chopping bits off the side or adding bits to the bottom.

Stitch gauges or tensions are generally written in terms of numbers of stitches and rows necessary to knit a 10 × 10 cm square when a specified needle is used. A specific pattern stitch (for example, stocking stitch or moss stitch) is also given because tensions vary between stitch patterns. By knitting a tension square or swatch, you not only find out whether your tension is correct for the pattern, but also you have an opportunity to learn the stitch pattern more readily because the piece of knitting is small and progresses quickly.

If your completed tension square is too wide, your knitting is too loose and you should use a smaller knitting needle size. If the square is too small and your knitting too tight, change needles for a larger size. One needle size smaller or larger makes a difference of one stitch every 5 cm (2 in.).

It is possible to use a different yarn from that specified in the pattern without necessarily altering stitch numbers if the yarns being interchanged knit up to the same gauge. If you wish to use a different yarn weight to that specified, a commercial pattern will be of less value in the pursuit of accurate stitch numbers.

Yarn ball bands sometimes provide helpful information regarding stitch gauges.

A variation in tension within a garment will result in an uneven appearance. If this is the effect you require, change your needle size or deliberately alternate pulling the yarn tighter and letting it run more loosely.

Cotton has a tendency to "shift" while it is being knitted. To correct this when working stocking stitch, change the needle size on the purl row.

WHAT IS THE RIGHT TENSION?

Knitting results in a stretch fabric. The amount of flexibility required and the intended use of the fabric assist you in deciding which needle size is best for your creation. For example, a heavy winter coat may be knitted on smaller needles than those recommended on the ball band, to minimise wind vents. A lacy shawl has to support little of its own weight, so you

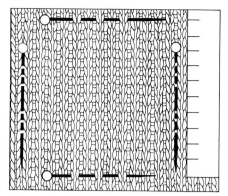

Place pins 10 cm apart and count the numbers of stitches and rows between the pins to work out the formula.

may choose to knit it on larger needles. However it is worth noting the following:

° Very tight knitting tends to be stiff and is likely to shrink in the wash.

° Very loose knitting tends to pill more, and it stretches in the wash.

° Just-right knitting tends to be accident prone and go astray in the knitting cupboard. You can't win!

To make things even more

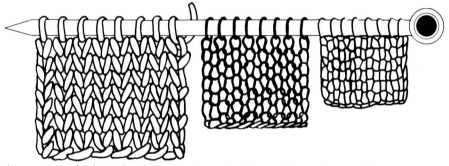

Any yarn can be knitted on any sized needles. Visual effect and wearability are deciding factors.

CHOOSING NEEDLE SIZES FOR YOUR OWN DESIGNS

The needle size used controls the stiffness of the knitted fabric. Suggested needle sizes for different yarn weights are as follows:

Yarn	Ribbing needles	Body needles
Fine-weight baby yarn	2 mm	2 –2½ mm
4-ply yarn	2 mm	2½–3¼ mm
Double-knitting yarn	3 mm	3¼–4½ mm
Triple-knitting yarn	4 mm	5–6 mm
Chunky and some mohair-type yarns	4 mm	5½–6½ mm
Heavy yarns	5 mm	7–9 mm

difficult, most people have a tendency to knit tightly when watching horror shows on television and loosely (even saggy) during soap operas. Ms Takes, for one, has turned this piece of valuable research to her advantage. She knits her ribbing (or welts) during dramas; sewing up she does during the news.

Note: Pilling is the rubbing together of fibres and the formation of hard little lumps of fibre on the surface of the garment. It occurs under the arms, along the sides of the garment and particularly where you do not want it. Soft, loosely twisted yarns are more prone to pilling than hard twist yarns. Pills can be removed by careful hairdressing of the garment with small scissors when the operator is in a sober state. Jersey shavers are available for removing pills from fine knitting.

CALCULATING STITCH NUMBERS

For any garment of a precise size you wish to make, do a tension square or swatch with the needles and in the stitch pattern you intend using.

If you intend using only one yarn and one needle size for the body of the garment, it will be relatively simple to work out the number of stitches to cast on. Choose the needles and yarn that will give the garment the appropriate amount of flexibility, and knit a sample square. Cast on enough stitches to cover a good 10 cm without counting the stitches at the extreme edges of the square. The larger the swatch, the more accurate the initial measurements and the more accurate the size of the finished garment.

If the design includes a range of yarn weights, knit the

swatch in the main or average thickness of yarn. If the yarn thicknesses vary widely but are repeated throughout the design, make a sample sufficiently large so the changes in yarn average themselves out. Such a swatch should measure about 15 × 15 cm.

Let's assume this swatch is knitted in stocking stitch. Place a pin vertically between two stitches, then place another pin parallel and exactly 10 cm away. It may or may not lie between stitches. Don't stretch the knitting or move the pin so that it lies between stitches if it does not do so naturally, regardless of how inviting a solution it may seem to be. A half stitch left uncalculated may cause your final measurements to be several centimetres out.

Count the number of stitches between the two pins. This is the first part of the formula necessary to work out the number of stitches to be cast on. Note this down as follows: 10 cm = x stitches.

The second part of the formula involves working out the required finished width of the garment piece in centimetres or inches.

Taking measurements If the yarns you have chosen are thick, don't measure yourself but measure a garment that feels nice when worn. If you don't have a garment of ideal size, measure yourself, but allow plenty of space for breathing and comfort. "Knitwit" patterns are a good source of measurements with built-in comfort spacing. They are particularly valuable if you are planning an unusual sleeve shaping or construction. Remember that they include seam allowances, which you will not need unless you intend sewing up the garment with

the back stitch method (see Chapter 8, Finishing).

Useful measurements are shown in the diagrams below.

Note: Some useful information on sleeve and armhole measurements may be found in the section on setting in sleeves (Chapter 7, Finishing).

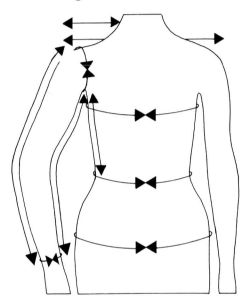

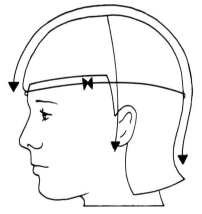

Back to the formula.

Let's assume the required hip measurement is 100 cm (40 in.). This means the front width of the jersey must be 50 cm (20 in.). Let's also assume that the number of stitches required to cover 10 cm is 15 (measured from the tension sample). The number of stitches required to cover 50 cm will be five times that in the 10 cm sample swatch, or 5 × 15.

For quick reference:

1. Garment piece measures X cm (total A).
2. Tension sample = X stitches per 10 cm (total B).
3. Divide X cm by 10 (total C, or number of 10 cm blocks per width). Simply move the decimal point one place to the left.
4. Total B × Total C = number of stitches per garment piece.

This formula is relevant only for the particular yarn, needles and stitch pattern used in the sample.

Now for the exciting part for the knitter with a well-developed sense of adventure. If a precise fit doesn't count in your designs, you can forsake the tension-square ritual. Just take your age, double it and cast on that number of stitches! If that doesn't look right, cast on a few more — or, subtract a lot if you're expecting a telegram from the Queen!

BANDS OR WELTS

If the width of the main body of the garment and the ribbing follow the usual proportions, they will be knitted on the same number of stitches. That is, if you need 80 stitches to obtain the correct front

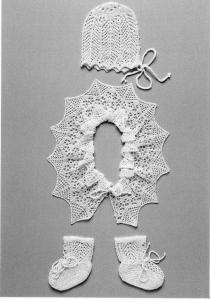

Margaret Stove's fine knitting shows technical expertise and New Zealand flora.

measurement, 80 stitches will also be appropriate for the ribbing. A transition from ribbing to stocking stitch naturally creates a small puff, as does a transition from ribbing to a lacey stitch. If you want a blouson effect with tight ribbing, add extra stitches evenly across the body — lots of extra stitches for a very full blouson; very few for a gentle puff.

Bands or welts do not necessarily have to be knitted in ribbing. Garter stitch, moss stitch and rolled stocking stitch make a nice change. Garter stitch pushes out the knitting a little, so it may be necessary to cast on slightly fewer stitches (about 10 per cent less) and add the extra after knitting the band.

Another option is to knit the bands sideways and attach them when the main body of the garment is finished. This allows adjustments and vertical stripes to be knitted easily. To

Bands are generally an area of unexplored design potential. This band uses the intarsia technique and retains its elasticity.   TC

add further interest, leave the side seams unstitched and add buttons or ties.

Loose bands can be a nuisance, needing to be rolled up at the cuffs and tending to go wavy at the bottom. Well-fitting cuffs, lower bands and neck often improve a design and the comfort of the garment. For information on how to fix sloppy bands, necks and cuffs on a completed garment see Chapter 9, Disasters.

You may actually plan a sloppy look or loose-fitting edges in your design. Moss stitch or versions of it are good for such edges because they do not roll and are complete in themselves.

Elastic cast on for 1 × 1 ribbing Use knitting needles two sizes larger than those used for the ribbing and some contrasting coloured yarn. Cast on *half* the number of stitches required.

Row 1: Knit
Row 2: Purl
Row 3: Knit
Row 4: Purl
Change to the yarn required for the ribbing.
Row 5: Knit
Row 6: Purl
Change to the required needles for ribbing and knit the first stitch. With the left hand needle pick up from the back of the work the main-colour loop between the two stitches where it joins the contrasting yarn and purl that stitch. Knit the next stitch from the left hand needle, pick up the next main-colour loop and purl it. Continue to the end of the row. Pull out the contrast yarn. If an even number of stitches is required an extra stitch must be made as the last stitch in the row does not have a loop below it. Continue in rib.

Elastic cast off for 1 × 1 ribbing This technique is similar to grafting. Use a wool needle or tapestry sewing needle with a rounded tip. Hold the knitting needle with the stitches on in your left hand. Thread a wool needle with a length of matching yarn and hold this in your right hand.

Begin by passing the wool needle through the first stitch knitwise and slipping that stitch off the knitting needle. Miss the next stitch. Pass the wool needle through the next stitch (a knit stitch) purlwise but leave it on the knitting needle. Go purlwise through the stitch that was missed and take it off. Take the wool needle round the back of your work and bring it between the first and second stitch on the knitting needle then go knitwise through the second stitch and leave it on. Repeat this process to the end of the row. After the first two stitches all other stitches should have been passed through twice, once knitwise and once purlwise.

EDGES

Scarves and ties knitted in stocking stitch often require an especially worked flat edge to avoid curling at the sides. Curling of stocking stitch or stocking stitch-based designs can be prevented by knitting a double garter stitch selvedge edge as follows:

° With the right side facing, slip the first stitch through the back of the stitch, not the front. This twists the stitch. Keep the yarn at the back of the work and knit the next stitch. Work to within the last two stitches, then knit these.

° With the wrong side facing, repeat the first row exactly.

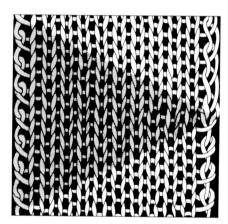

SHAPING

For a female, generally there is no need to increase or decrease up the sides, because hip and shoulder measurements are usually the same. For a male, add extra width to the sides by gradually increasing the number of stitches until there are about 10 per cent more than the original number cast on.

Make the back about 3 cm (1 in.) higher than the front to solve the problem of choking the wearer in the front and exposing the back of the neck. This is particularly valuable for males as they generally do not have a bust to pull down the front neckline!

Decreasing Decreasing on the right-hand side of a piece of knitting is often done by knitting two stitches together at the beginning of a right-side-facing row. It is usually written in abbreviated form in patterns as K.2 tog. There are several methods of obtaining a mirror image of this effect for use on the left-hand edge of the knitting:

° Knit until two stitches remain, slip one, knit one, then pass the slipped stitch over the knitted stitch. This is written in abbreviated form as follows: Sl.1, K.1, p.s.s.o.

° Knit along the row until two stitches remain, then knit the remaining two stitches together through the backs of the loops.

° Knit along the row until two stitches remain, slip these two stitches knitwise, then put the tip of the left-hand needle into them and knit them together from this position. This method is the most accurate mirror image of knitting two stitches together on the left-hand side.

Double decreasing To decrease two stitches at the edge of the knitting proceed as follows:

° Slip two stitches together as if knitting them, knit the next one, then pass the two slipped stitches over.

Increasing Stitches may be increased invisibly within a row (i.e. without creating a small hole beneath each new stitch) by following the method outlined:

° When working a knit row, put the right-hand needle from front to back through the top of the stitch *below* the next one to be knitted and knit it in the usual way. Then knit the next stitch on the left-hand needle.

° When working a purl row, put the right-hand needle from back to front into the top of the stitch *below* the next one to be purled and purl it in the usual way. Then purl the next stitch on the left-hand needle.

A boat-necked opening running right down the sleeves with buttoned closures.

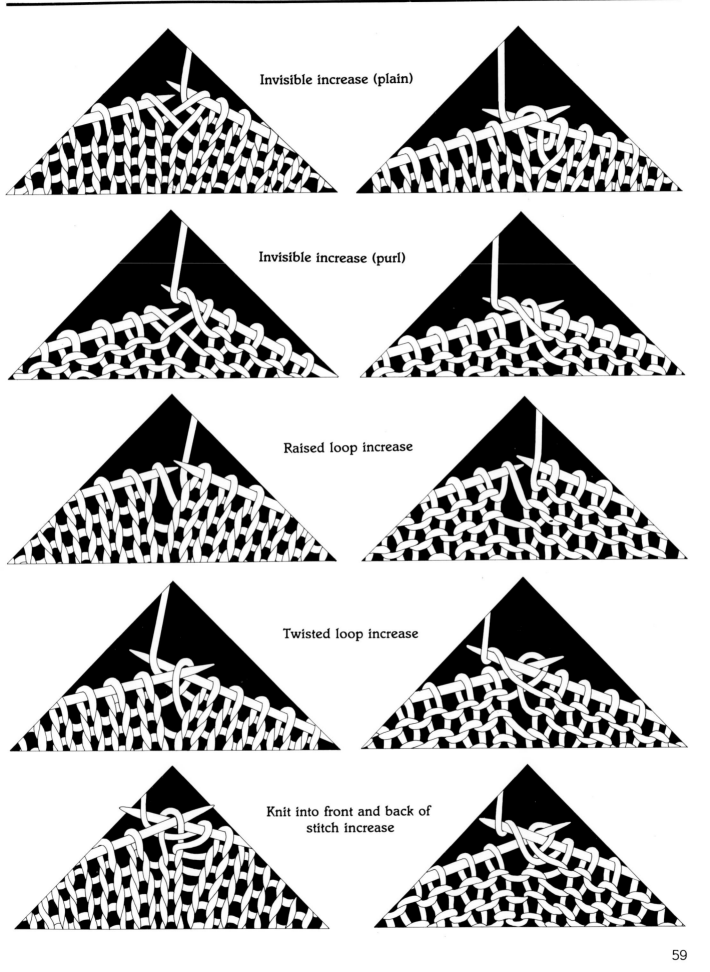

Invisible increase (plain)

Invisible increase (purl)

Raised loop increase

Twisted loop increase

Knit into front and back of stitch increase

DIFFERENT WEIGHTS OF YARN IN A ROW

In the vast majority of designs there is only one weight of yarn in the garment. This is generally advisable because similar yarns will not pull down, push out or pull in, all of which can occur if you use a variety of weights in a single garment or even in a single row. If all the colours and textures you need are not available in the same ply, combine several finer yarns and knit them as a single strand. This technique is discussed further in Chapter 3, Yarns.

Informal designs may deliberately employ uneven weights of yarn to create specific effects (for instance, a concertina appearance). If a row of thick yarn is followed by a row of thin yarn and this sequence is repeated, the knitting will be wavy at the edges. Such effects can be used to great advantage on collars, frills, sleeves and so on (including, of course, gills for fish, if you happen to be knitting one).

If you want a straight edge but still wish to use combinations of thick and thin yarns in one garment, it is possible to even out the wavy effect to some extent. Different techniques are available, depending on whether the

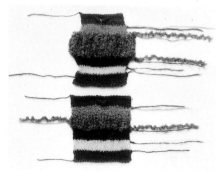

Concertina effects may be eliminated by the addition of stitches and by changing needle sizes.

design requires a complete row in thick yarn then a complete row in thin yarn, or whether the yarns are changed more randomly.

Complete rows in different yarn
Use one or a combination of several of these techniques, according to what suits the design.
° Knit the rows of finer-than-average yarns on larger needles.
° Knit the thicker-than-average yarns on smaller needles.
° Add more stitches evenly across the row when changing to finer yarn and change to larger needles. Decrease these extra stitches when you change back to the thicker yarn.
° Decrease the number of stitches when working with thicker yarns (perhaps by knitting two together). This works well when the yarn changes part way through a row. Add them on afterwards, when the next row of thinner yarn is worked.
° Choose a lacey, holey stitch for finer yarns.
° Choose a slip stitch or cable stitch for thicker yarns. Such stitches actually pull in the edges of the knitting effectively, but they also thicken the fabric further, accentuating the weight difference between finer and thicker yarns. This may be the effect you desire.

The use of any of the techniques outlined above makes careful, supportive washing extra important.

The information above applies also to changes in decorative stitches while using the same yarn. If you change from stocking stitch to a slip stitch or cable design without making any adjustments, and then back to stocking stitch,

your knitting will concertina in and out. Simply by adding some extra stitches across the width and decreasing them when reverting to stocking stitch, you can neutralise this effect.

Part rows in different yarns
These techniques are used to compensate for different weights of yarn in a garment when they occur in blocks or small areas rather than over complete rows.
° Knit each yarn area as a separate section and sew sections together. This technique is useful if you wish to pad and quilt areas of finer yarns within a garment (see Chapter 7, Finishing). The sewing process can be used to add further decoration — perhaps leather thonging, fine lace or contrasting yarns. Gaps may be deliberately left to make a pattern of holes between the different yarns.
° Knit extra "half rows" with the finer yarns, resulting in more rows of the finer yarn in relation to thicker yarns. (If the difference in yarn weights is extreme, it is probably easier to knit them as separate sections; but if the difference is minor, the above technique is useful.) A half row is an extra row on only one side of a garment piece. Half rows never seem to cover exactly half a row, but let's continue. To make a half row, knit for the required distance across the piece in finer yarn. Turn the work. Slip the first stitch off the left-hand needle, then continue knitting back to the beginning of the row. If you like, knit right across the next row in finer yarn. Neatly hidden in the knitting will be two extra half rows. If you want the turning point

of the half row to be a visible part of the design, make a lovely hole by not bothering to slip the first stitch on the return row.

There is another method of making a half row without a hole. Knit to the point where you wish to turn, slip the next stitch, bring the yarn to the front of the work and slip the stitch back onto the left-hand needle. Turn the work, then knit (or purl) back to the beginning of the row. This technique is useful for fully fashioned shaping of busts, socks and shoulder lines.

GRAFTING

Grafting is the invisible joining of two pieces of knitting with a needle and wool thread. The method varies according to the type of stitch used to knit the two pieces.

Stocking stitch, knit side: The two pieces of knitting are held with the stitches to be joined facing each other and directly lined up with each other. They are slipped off the knitting needles a few at a time and the wool thread is used to form a new row of stitches that join the two pieces of knitting.

Stocking stitch, purl side: Simply work the join on the knit side, as outlined above, and use the reverse side as the right side; or, line up the purl stitches alternately and sew through each stitch, duplicating the shape of the purl stitches, as shown.

Garter stitch: This stitch is a little trickier to graft because a purl row must be joined to a knit row to make the invisible seam. Before starting to sew the seam, just make sure that one piece of knitting ends with a purl row and the other finishes on a knit row. Line up the two pieces so that a knit stitch lies between each purl stitch, and use the wool thread to form a joining row of stitches, as shown.

Knit 2, purl 2 ribbing: For grafting this stitch use a combination of the first two methods. Ensure that the order and width of the ribbed stitches matches exactly on the two pieces of knitting.

BUTTONHOLES

Buttonholes may be worked in several ways, three of which are outlined below:

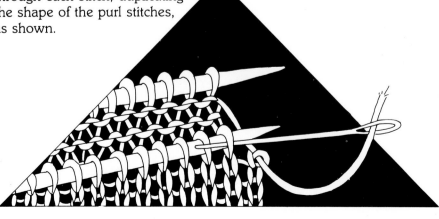

Eyelet buttonhole: A small buttonhole, suitable for small buttons or threaded ribbon. On the right side of the knitting, work to the buttonhole position, pass the yarn around the needle (to make a stitch), then knit two stitches together. Purl the made stitch in the next row in the normal manner. To finish the buttonhole, sew around it with thread when the knitting is completed, if you prefer.

Horizontal buttonhole: On the right side of the knitting, knit to the required site of the buttonhole and cast off a few stitches (according to the size required). Continue knitting to the end of the row. On the return row, the same number of stitches are cast on over the cast off stitches.

Vertical buttonhole: To make a long buttonhole, suitable for thin, vertically placed buttons, divide the work where the buttonhole is required (that is, knit along to the buttonhole site, turn the work and continue knitting on the set of stitches now on the left-hand needle for the required length). Then join the yarn to the second set of stitches and work the same number of rows on these stitches. When both sides are equal in length, join up the hole at the top by knitting across both sets of stitches.

KNITTING AT ANGLES

An intarsia effect without the associated tangles (see Chapter 6, Intarsia) can be achieved by knitting separate sections on different angles and sewing them together.

Use the formula outlined on page 55 to work out the number of stitches needed from point A to point B. The completed lower section of your knitting may provide a ready-made swatch upon which to work out the formula.

In the example illustrated, the gauge is 20 stitches per 10 cm in the lower portion. Line A–B measures 28 cm. You will need 2.8 10 cm portions to span the distance between point A and point B. The number of stitches required is therefore 20 × 2.8 stitches, or 56.

If you continued knitting straight after casting on and picking up 56 stitches, you would finish with a rather weird shape. To adjust the edges in this case, it would probably be necessary to decrease one stitch every front-facing row on the left-hand side and increase one stitch every front-facing row on the right-hand side. If the

New stitches are picked up along the edges of each block.

cast-off angle on the original piece of knitting is steep, you will probably have to decrease one stitch every row on the left-hand side and increase one stitch each row on the right-hand side.

When you reach the point where the right-hand edge is the correct length for the garment, the left-hand edge will be too short. It will be necessary to continue simultaneously building up the left-hand side and squaring off the top. This is done by following the technique you have been using for the left-hand edge, while casting off one stitch every one or two rows on the right-hand side. (Up to this point you will have been increasing on the right-hand side.)

THREE-DIMENSIONAL KNITTING

Using the formula discussed on page 55, it is possible to work out an appropriate number of stitches to pick up and knit *out* a shape vertically, horizontally or diagonally.

Let's assume your gauge is 10 rows and seven stitches per 5 cm. Let's also assume that the protruding shape will be knitted in the same yarn as that used for the main body of the work and that you want it to be of the same tension.

If the required shape is to be attached *horizontally* to the main body of the garment, pick up stitches one for one. (Use a smaller needle for picking up stitches if you like — it's easier.) For example, for a 5 cm flap, pick up seven stitches over seven stitches of the garment piece. The correct number of stitches for a *vertically* attached shape, say a 5 cm square door, will be seven stitches over 5 cm or 10 rows. Just skip a row every now and again.

To work out how many stitches to pick up to make a *diagonal* flap, place pins 5 cm apart (in this case). Pick up the seven stitches evenly over the 5 cm measurement (probably over 8 rows).

Once you've started the shape, knit out, twist it and knit back in if you like, or just cast off after a few rows, leaving a

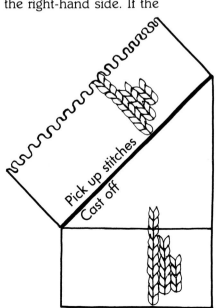

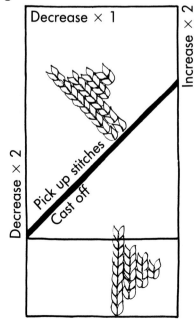

little decorative flap or door. Possibly add a button to make a real opening door.

SIMPLE TEXTURED STITCHES

Garter stitch, moss stitch and reverse stocking stitch are the basis of textured knitting. Although stocking stitch is smooth, when used in Aran designs it is twisted and cleverly combined with garter and moss stitch in such a way that a sculptured effect is created.

Simple textured stitch patterns are ideal for novelty yarns because they force out into the limelight the fluff or crunchy, interesting bits of such yarns.

When doing Aran work, check the reverse side of your knitting. It often provides pleasant surprises in the form of reverse sculptured patterns which you might like to incorporate in future designs.

Four yarns knitted in stocking stitch.

The reverse side of the same yarns showing the more textured appearance and consequently more effective use of textured yarns.

GATHERS AND PUCKERS

You can create a blouson effect

in a garment by rapidly increasing across a whole row, by knitting one, making one stitch, into every stitch. After the stitch numbers have been doubled in this way, an accordian effect can be obtained by immediately decreasing back to the original number of stitches. This can be done by knitting two together all the way along the next row.

To make the knitting puff out, as in a puffed sleeve, delay the rapid decrease by knitting more ordinary rows between the increasing and decreasing rows. You can create an effect reminiscent of the sleeves of knights and ladies of old by duplicating puffs over a large area of the knitting. This can be further enhanced by your choice of colours or by doing a split layer of knitting in heavier yarn over a finer, possibly lacy, layer of knitting.

LADDERS

Holes can become ladders, and ladders are wonderful, too! A dropped stitch will ladder all the way to the cast-on row. If, when it is nearly completed, a summer top looks as if it will be too small in width, you can add extra width by the judicious dropping of stitches to make a lovely lacy stitch.

Controlled ladders In order to stop a ladder in a certain place, it is necessary to make an extra stitch that will eventually become the ladder. On the row where you want the ladder to stop, knit into the bar between two stitches and make an extra stitch. A small hole will form at the point of introduction of the new stitch, so you will be able to tell where it was done. It is easy to forget where you planned to end a ladder.

Now knit as many rows as

you want to give length to the ladder (three, five, 10, 20 or whatever) and drop the extra stitch. Voila! The result will be a leaf-shaped ladder if only a few rows have been dropped, or a long, fine ladder if it reaches down through many rows.

SLIP STITCH DESIGNS

The effect of Fairisle can be achieved by slipping stitches instead of carrying different coloured yarns behind the work and knitting them in at intervals. In slip stitch designs only one colour per row is used but at intervals the colour used in the previous row is lifted into the new row by slipping the stitch on to the right-hand needle without knitting it. A basic requirement of slip-stitch designs is the changing of colours for every row in which stitches are to be lifted or slipped. If this is not done, the result will be an Aran or textured effect instead of a mock Fairisle appearance.

Slipping stitches pulls in the sides of the knitting and reduces its elasticity. If you are planning lots of slipped stitches, add a few extra stitches at the beginning of the knitting to compensate.

You can create a brick-wall effect by slipping the same stitch over three or more rows while knitting the remaining stitches in reverse stocking stitch. Make the "mortar" a different colour from the "bricks" to develop this idea even further. When knitting this design it is necessary to put the "mortar" yarn behind the "brick" yarn when both yarns are being carried behind the work.

Keep looking at what you are doing with a critical eye; train your other eye to look out for possible new inventions!

HOLES

Holes are wonderful! The most basic hole of a controlled nature can be made by simply knitting two stitches together and putting the yarn over the top of the needle, making a new stitch to replace the one you devoured. The principle of hole-making is to provide enough yarn in one row to make wonderful holes by dropping stitches in the next.

Lovely, long, loopy areas can be made by winding the yarn around the needle several times between stitches on the first row and dropping all the extra loops in the next. These loops may be slipped for several rows, then knitted again in the normal way. Twisted, elongated stitches are made by twisting the loop before knitting it back on the normal row. They may be twisted as many times as you like.

CABLES

Cables are created when stitches are moved out of position, either on their own or in groups. To make the twisting and shifting of stitches easier, short, two-pointed cable needles are used. Cables are usually knitted in stocking stitch on a reverse stocking stitch or moss stitch background.

Make a basic cable as follows:
Row 1: Purl 3, knit 6, purl 3 to the end of the pattern section.
Row 2: Knit 3, purl 6, knit 3 to the end.
Row 3: Purl 3, knit 6, purl 3, to the end.
Row 4: Repeat second row.
Row 5: Purl 3, place the next 3 stitches on a cable needle at the back of the work, knit the next 3 stitches, knit the 3 stitches on the cable needle, purl 3, and so on.
Row 6: Repeat second row.

The cable can be made to cross over in the opposite direction by leaving the stitches on the cable needle at the front instead of the back of the work. The basic cable can be varied in an infinite number of ways. Test your ingenuity in cable-making with an experimental sampler!

If you don't have a cable needle on hand, use a match for shifting one or two stitches, but watch out for splinters. No cable needle is necessary if you are quick and are working with a small number of stitches. Stitches are not malicious things; they will just wait around for you if you don't leave them for too long.

Travelling cables It is possible to make cables that travel freely across the front and even go behind the knitting to resurface elsewhere. Try treating those stitches you intend cabling as separate from the background. Knit a few extra rows on those stitches alone and they will seem to take on a life of their own. Knit an extra 10 cm on those stitches by turning the work in much the same way as you do when knitting a bobble. The resulting flap can be split into separate sections and plaited or cabled within itself, then moved across the front of your work. Join it in whenever you want.

It is advisable to keep a track of the original stitch numbers.

Orange Un-Jersey, designed and knitted by Lee Anderson and modelled by Allana Woodford.

If you have pinched a bunch of six stitches for a cable from one place in the knitting, you may need to invent six stitches behind that spot to fill the space.

When feeding the cable back into the knitting in a different place, you may need to get rid of the extra stitches there. This can be done by laying the cable-carrying needle in front of the left-hand needle. Hold these two needles together as if they were one. Knit two together, one off each left-hand needle onto the right-hand needle.

If the cable is different in colour to the background, effective decorative, free-form cables can be made to travel across the knitting, almost as if they were knitted separately and stitched on afterwards. Of course, that's a good idea in itself. By knitting lots of separate tubes and plaiting, twisting and even knotting them, you can puzzle your friends and influence people.

Separate knitted and plaited or cabled strips sewn around necks, cuffs and edges make a nice change on a garment. Open lattice-work effects can be created by splitting up all the stitches and weaving the resulting long strips of knitting. The design potential from this idea is limitless.

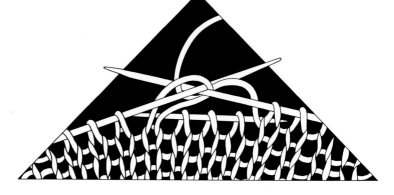

NOPES, BOBBLES AND FRENCH KNOTS

Bobbles Bobbles are made by repeatedly increasing into a single stitch . . . the yarn used has nowhere to go but out! Depending on the number of times you increase into one stitch, you can make anything from a huge bobble-mountain to a shy, tentative bobble.

This is how to make a very normal, average-looking bobble:
Row 1: Knit along the row to the chosen bobble site. Knit into the next stitch as many times as you like (say five times). You may have noticed that the knit stitches keep turning into a long loop. One way to fix this is to knit into the front of the stitch, then the back, then the front, then the back and so on. Alternatively, knit one into the front of the stitch, put the yarn forward and over the top, making the next loop, then knit into the front of the stitch again, put the yarn forward and over, and so on.
Row 2: After knitting repeatedly into the starting bobble stitch, turn the work and purl those five (or whatever) stitches. Turn the work again.
Row 3: Knit the five bobble stitches. On this row you may prefer to slip the first and last of the five stitches. Turn the work again.
Row 4: Purl the five stitches.

Turn the work.
Row 5: If you are ready to close up the bobble, knit three stitches together or all five, if you can manage it, but they will be tight. Knitting into the back of the stitch is easier than knitting into the front. Knit together the last two stitches, leaving only two stitches. Pass one over the top of the other.

Now continue knitting the original row until you come to the next bobble site, but remember to pull tight the first stitch after the bobble you have just made, to avoid forming a hole.

Instead of stocking stitch, bobbles may be worked in garter stitch or even moss stitch. After knitting sufficient rows over the initial increased stitches, you can decrease back to the original starting stitch as quickly or as slowly as you like. Symmetrical bobbles are generally increased and decreased in the same number of rows (that is, if the increasing for the bobble is done all in one row, it is decreased back to the original starting stitch in one row, to match).

The trick to knitting successful bobbles lies in the first flat stitch knitted after the formation of the bobble. This stitch must be pulled tightly to avoid a large hole forming behind the bobble. Small ones are inevitable and may be designated finger-warmers, should anyone ask. If you really don't need finger-warmers, try slipping the two outside stitches on one of the bobble rows to assist the bobble to curl inwards.

Bobbles-on-bobbles are what you get if you start making a new bobble before finishing the first one. If a wart is required on a bobble, this is a good way to make one.

Noses are what you get when you forget to decrease a bobble back to the original number of stitches. This increases the number of stitches in a row dramatically, but they can always be got rid of later and you may have invented a brand-new pattern!

It *is* possible to knit bobbles without turning the work if you learn to knit backwards — true!

A formal bobble (for evening wear!) *Row 1*: Knit along to the bobble site. Take the yarn forward to the front of the work and over the needle. Knit into the front of the next stitch. Put the yarn forward and over the top again, and knit into the front of the same stitch again.

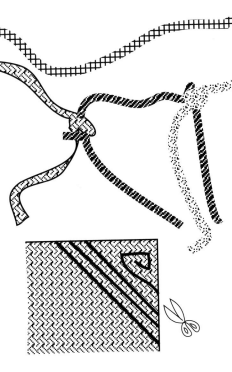

Put the yarn forward and knit into the stitch one more time. You should have a loop plus five additional loops from the one stitch.

Row 2: Turn the work. Slip the first stitch purlwise onto the right-hand needle. Purl the five stitches.

Row 3: Turn the work. Slip the first stitch knitwise onto the right-hand needle and knit five stitches.

Row 4: Turn. Purl two stitches together, three times.

Row 5: Turn. Slip one stitch knitwise. Knit two together and pass the slipped stitch over.

One stitch now remains on the needle, and you are ready to continue on your way.

Nopes, or baby bobbles To make baby bobbles for more conservative projects, simply make lots of stitches from one stitch, then pass all the new stitches over the last stitch formed.

French knots French knots are usually knitted on a stocking stitch background.

First, knit a few rows of stocking stitch until you are at the place where you want the knots to start. It takes two pattern rows to complete them, then more stocking stitch is worked to the point where another row of French knots is required.

French knots can be worked in more than one colour. A nice effect can be attained by combining the textured French knots with Fairisle and knitting them in three colours, one for the background and two for the

knots. In the following example they will be done in pink and red on a blue background, like little roses. The colours are referred to as B (blue), P (pink) and R (red).

Knit the initial rows of blue stocking stitch. Be ready to begin the knots on a plain row.

Row 1: Knit 3B, 1R, 3B, 1R to the end (actually, any odd number of stitches can be worked between the red stitches that start the French knots).

Row 2: Purl 3B, knit 1P, purl 3B, knit 1 P to the end. To weave in the unused yarn and get it in the right place, carry the red along the back of the work and, just before knitting the pink stitch, put it forward between the stitches, knit the pink stitch, then move it back again behind the stitch until it is required.

An odd number of stitches between the knots allows you to offset the next row of knots. Carry the colours up the side of the knitting until they are required for the next line of

knots. You may decide to begin them on a purl row. If so, knit the pattern rows as follows:

Row 1: Purl 3B, purl 1R, purl 3B, purl 1R to the end.

Row 2: Knit 3B, purl 1P, knit 3B, purl 1P to the end.

Any buckling that occurs between the knots can be avoided by stretching the work while carrying the unused colours behind it. Should you wish to accentuate the puckering between the knots, making a smocking effect, tightly pull the yarn being carried between the knots.

FRINGING

By tying together and knitting scraps of yarn you can achieve a colourful, hairy look on the surface of your knitting. Coordination of scraps can result in a rich, textured effect, even within a limited colour range. You don't necessarily need to use yarns of the same type, nor need the materials be restricted to yarns. Combinations of fabrics and yarn, dyed silk, bias-cut strips of your favourite ex-parrot (I mean, ex-dress!) all make wonderful knitted nonsense.

Alternatively, fringing may be added to the surface after the knitting is complete by hooking in lengths of yarn with a crochet hook. A full flounce results from hooking pieces of fringing while the garment is the right way up. A more subdued, droopy fringe is obtained by hooking pieces of yarn while the garment is held upside down.

Above: This garment has sections knitted on an angle sewn to normally knitted sections. **Left:** Detail showing French knots on a background of gold and brown fleece dyed handspun wool. **Below:** Knotted and knitted silk fabric strips with added red fringing and embroidery.

CHAPTER FIVE

FAIRISLE

From a distance Fairisle seems to be made up of mottled colours in horizontal stripes, yet close inspection reveals complex patterns within patterns, carefully executed through colour. Generally, two coloured yarns are carried the complete length of each row, surfacing in the stocking stitch colour work pattern every five stitches or so. In Fairisle, complexity and subtlety are prized. Traditional patterns may have a substantial history and clan identity.

TENSION

One of the greatest moments of frustration known to knitters is when a marathon Fairisle effort has its debut and proves to be . . . oh no, too tight! Usually the cause is carrying the wool too tightly across the back of the work, resulting in puckering and lack of elasticity. This can be particularly fatal for the life of a piece of knitting if no allowance is made for the fact that Fairisle is less elastic than standard knitting anyway. To guard against such an unfortunate happening, it is probably a good idea to add to each side a few extra stitches that could be sewn into the seams if the extra width is not required.

If your cupboard contains examples of Fairisle knitting that are too tight or too puckered to wear, take heart — Fairisle liberation is here! Take them out of the closet and turn to the disasters section of the plot.

The key to achieving exactly the right tension for Fairisle is to knit too loose deliberately. While carrying the yarn across the back of the work, stretch apart all the stitches on the right-hand needle. When the work is returned to a relaxed position, the resulting loop of yarn will ease itself into the knitting, allowing you to move and stretch in the garment and to put it on without difficulty.

Loose carrying of unused yarn can be exaggerated to the extent that a different problem arises. Long loops just love to catch themselves around fingers when the wearer is pulling on the garment in a hurry. A happy compromise is to carry the yarn loosely, but over fewer rather than too many stitches. A distance of around 2 cm or about five stitches is good.

Try taking the above into account at the design stage. A pattern in which both colours are carried over a distance of only five stitches is challenging to devise, but rewarding. If you require a longer gap between the recurrence of a particular colour, twist the yarn around the main colour every few stitches at the back of the work. If the space between recurring colours is too great, there is a danger of sacrificing elasticity, not to mention wasting yarn by carrying it right across the back of the work. In such cases the intarsia technique is likely to be more useful (see Chapter 6).

FAIRISLE GRAPHS AND CHARTS

Fairisle designs can be knitted from written colour instructions, or, more commonly, from information presented on a chart or graph. In commercial Fairisle charts the bottom right-hand corner represents the first stitch of a Fairisle design. This is fine for knitters who are right handed. Left-handed knitters can start from the bottom left-hand corner of such a chart without too much difficulty, if working solely from the chart, without written instructions (which follow the right-handed method). Fairisle charts are read from the bottom upwards and in a zig-zag motion. Even-numbered rows are read from left to right and odd-numbered rows from right to left. Fairisle work is traditionally knitted in the round, on circular needles. This method is advantageous in that the front of the work always faces the knitter and charts are read from right to left in every row.

Each square (or rectangle, if you use knitters' graph paper, in which the proportions are adjusted for the shape of the knitted stitch) in a Fairisle chart represents an individual stitch in the knitting. Each row or round of the knitting is represented by one line on the chart. A section that is to be repeated right across a row may be all that is shown.

Symbols may be used in Fairisle charts instead of the specified colours, to decrease printing costs. They may also be used if the pattern includes two similar colours that may be confused with each other. When designing your own Fairisle patterns, while at the experimental stage, you, too, may choose to use symbols.

After deciding on the pattern, you may like to try different colour combinations, as follows. Make up several charts using symbols such as spots, diagonal lines and crosses to represent various colours, then colour over the top of the symbols with different colour options.

If you wish, borrow ideas and patterns from commercial charts and combine them or perhaps incorporate some of your own in a design; it is helpful to choose only those with the same repeat number. To work out the repeat number, count the stitches from the beginning of the pattern. If stitch nine is the same as stitch one, if stitch 10 is the same as stitch two and so on, the repeat number is eight. This means that eight stitches are required to complete a shape or section of the design. In a repeat design of this nature, the recurring shape will finish *complete* at the end of a row and, as the knitting progresses, the shapes will appear exactly in line with each other vertically (see illustration).

If you try to mix a six-stitch repeat design with an eight-stitch repeat, you may find that there is a half or quarter of a shape at the right-hand side of the knitting and a complete shape at the left-hand side. This may not trouble you to distraction or

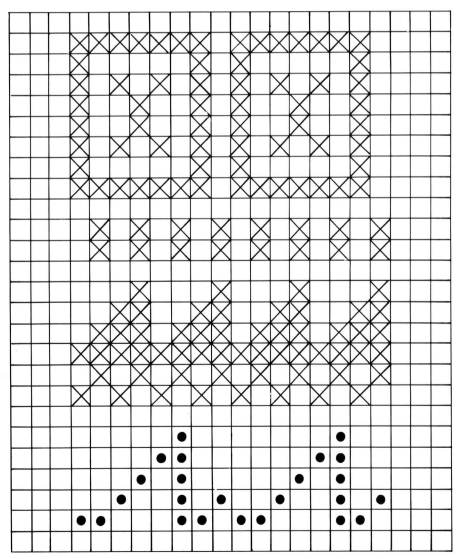

alcohol; you may even dub it a prime paradox, an informal formality, a disordered order. If it does worry you, decide upon a repeat number at the design stage and stick to it.

A repeat number of five stitches is a good one to begin with because it makes good triangles, a commonly used base design. An odd number of stitches is necessary for the base of an equilateral or isosceles triangle, but a right-angled triangle works equally well from an odd or even number of base stitches. If you try to knit an equilateral triangle from an even-numbered base, the point will not taper neatly to one stitch.

Graphing spots Fairisled spots can look very effective, but if you want them to be round, formal entities, as opposed to something resembling a batch of squashed tomatoes, you'll have to consider this at the graphing stage.

On standard graph paper each unit is a square, whereas the knitted unit, or stitch, is actually a flattened square or rectangle. A spot graphed as a circle on standard graph paper will knit up as a slightly squashed circle, whereas a spot graphed as a tallish oval will knit up to form a true spot. The bigger the spot, the more exaggerated the effect. If the width of the spot is only six stitches it will be flattened during knitting hardly at all. However, if the spot is 16 stitches wide it will need to be about 20 rows high to form a true circle. As a general rule,

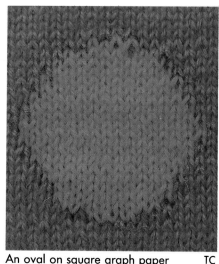

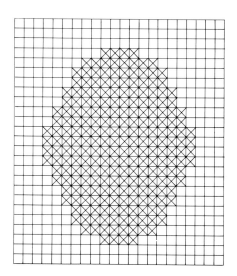

An oval on square graph paper knits up as a circle.　　TC

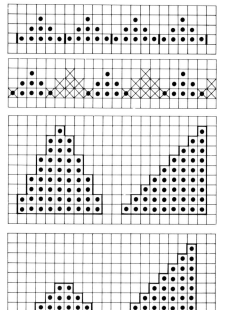

Pierrot, designed and knitted by Mary-Helen Eyre. By dividing different batch numbers of white with tiny triangles, the subtle colour change is acknowledged and used as an asset. The bow is knitted as a flap, a bobble and another flap all from a central point.

when using standard graph paper, draw the design a little taller than required.
Graphing words Graphs are especially useful when it is

Jay Farnsworth combines traditional images with richly coloured yarns.

necessary to fit a planned number of letters into a set number of stitches.

It can actually take more stitches and rows than you may first think to make a letter of the alphabet look normal.

(Try graphing just your initials in the space of 20 stitches and 20 rows.) The diagonal, upright and horizontal lines that form the letters of the alphabet have a habit of appearing different in Fairisle work, even when they are knitted over the same number of stitches. I've found that they can be made to appear equal by using three rows for a horizontal line, two stitches for a vertical line and four stitches for a diagonal line. A diagonal line on a very flat angle may have to be knitted over five or six stitches to appear equal in width to a two-stitch vertical line.

It is unlikely, but not impossible, that you would want to knit the statement in the accompanying illustration.

Should you wish to do so, it will be necessary to plan ahead so there *isn't* enough room for the whole sentence. Graphing it first is the obvious answer.

If you wish to put a child's name on a jersey over a limited number of stitches, it may also require graphing. It may be more interesting if the child draws his or her own name on a small "cartoon" (see Chapter 6, Intarsia). Children devise wonderful solutions for the problems of operating in cramped spaces, including using letters with elongated tails and allowing the words to spill over onto the sleeves.

Poetry jersey designed and machine knitted by Helen Rutherford.

FAIRISLE

DESIGNING YOUR OWN FAIRISLE

Incredibly intricate and subtle designs and colour changes can be worked using Fairisle. It can be as simple or as complex as you like, much like card games and other valuable endeavours. Two "games" you can play are what I call Strip Poker Fairisle, associated with bluffing, and Bridge Fairisle, which has more to do with masochism and suits cryptic crossword players and readers of crime novels.

Strip Poker Fairisle *Rules of the game:* Knit a tension swatch, work out the formula and number of stitches required (see page 55) or just use a pattern that works for the type of yarn you have chosen. Do the ribbing or hem, add more stitches for good luck and *go.* There are no rules, in fact.

If you get to the end of a row and find the pattern hasn't repeated exactly, disregard it joyfully. If, at the end of a row, there is no new wool waiting patiently, add a new colour, or slip all the stitches back onto the right-hand needle, or just knit another row using the colours you have, making bobbles along the way (see page 66) if plain knitting makes you sleepy. If you run out of a colour in the middle of a row, change colours. If you fancy a few rows of plain knitting (perhaps there's a good programme on television), just knit away and later add some beads or Swiss-darned decoration.

Advice to new players:
Try casting on enough stitches to knit the back and front at the same time. There are several advantages in this:
° Random changes will look terribly well organised, well planned and intricate

because they will appear exactly the same on the front and back and along the sides.
° When the knitting is long enough it can be split at the armhole opening to enable the back and front to be worked separately, allowing you to make the back yoke different from the front (in case you or the eager recipient can't tell one from the other!). If you are a formal sort of knitter and wish to continue the front and back the same, roll all the remaining colours into separate halves. Put one lot into a bag and hide it for the back; knit the rest into the front. In theory, you will be left with the right amount of matching colours for the back of the garment. However, according to Murphy's Law, it is likely that despite the best of efforts you will run out of each and every colour just before the end of a row. This could be put down to the fact that it is difficult to make two balls of yarn the same size exactly. One way of avoiding this problem is to knit the back first and, if there seems even the most remote possibility of running out of yarn for the front, change the design to a deep V neck.
° If you tire of Fairisling before the main body of the garment is finished, you can stop and do the rest in textured yarns or intarsia work or a plain stripe and block design, without having to reknit the front or back to match. If this idea appeals, work a little Fairisle on the sleeves, too, to pull the design together. By the time you have finished the front and back yoke you will probably be ready to tackle a slice of Fairisle once again.

° If your Fairisle turns out to be miles or kilometres too small and you have knitted both sides together, you can make the whole body into the back only and knit another front.

Bridge Fairisle *Rules of the game:* The rules for this complex but well planned tactical game are as challenging as they are restrictive. However, successful champions of Bridge Fairisle would deserve an honourary degree in mathematics from the University of Knitting if there were such a place.

Before beginning the game, knit a tension swatch, work out the formula and required numbers of stitches and rows (see page 55), then draw an outline of the garment on graph paper.
° Use only two colours in one row (one to five colours *may* be used, but two are the norm for most traditional Fairisle designs). The idea is to make the design appear even more complicated than it is by the clever use of colours changing row by row as much as within the row.
° Design the pattern so that only five or fewer stitches are knitted before a colour resurfaces. Twining in the floating colour at the back is an emergency measure only, for true fanatics.
° Plan to have the colours you require on the correct side when you need them. Draw arrows on the sides of the chart, showing the direction of the knitting and the end of each row, for easy reference. You will then be able to tell from a quick glance at the chart the whereabouts of the desired colour. If it was left at the left end of a row, the next row utilising that colour should begin at the left. If it

was used in a plain knitting row, it will be used next on a purl row.

° Advanced players may split the pairs of colours in a more complicated version of the game. Here's an example. The first plain row is knitted in red and blue. On the return purl row, the blue is left behind while the red is Fairisled with green. On the next plain row the green is taken back to the left side with a purple yarn. Here the original red is retrieved, a red and purple row is purled, then a blue and purple row is knitted back to the left-hand side. While all this is taking place, the motif or design is continued . . . wonderful fun!

° Use a range of repeat pattern sizes. It is definitely easier to limit yourself to a particular repeat pattern size and play around with that all the way up the garment; however, advanced players may wish to play a version of the game I call Multiple Bridge Fairisle. To play this game choose a number that is the multiple of several other smaller numbers. These must divide into the main number cleanly, with no remainders.

Take eight for example. With this repeat number you can knit patterns that repeat every eight stitches, every four stitches or every two stitches. This should be enough to satisfy most people. However, extremely advanced players may like to take into account the total number of stitches in their row. If it is 96, for example, the design could also be repeated in multiples of six, 12 and even 24 stitches (6 × 16 = 96; 12 × 8 = 96; 24 × 4 = 96). If, on the other hand, the total stitch

number was 80, neither six nor nine would repeat (divide into 80) exactly, but five and 10 would.

To sum up (excuse the pun), if the stitch total were 96, repeat designs could be made every two, four, six, eight, 12 and 24 stitches. All these repeats would result in a completed design at the end of a row. If the stitch total were 80, repeat designs could be made every two, four, five, eight, 10, 20 and 40 stitches.

If your stitch total is an uneven number like 71 you would be best advised to add one stitch or quietly lose one while no one is looking. Alternatively, you could defend such a total by claiming that you had planned to have buttons up one edge and needed an extra, spare stitch as an attachment point for the loops. Be warned, however, in claiming that the extra stitch is needed for a seam allowance. Most experienced competitors would realise that an extra stitch is needed each side for a backstitched seam.

° A pattern may repeat not only across a row, but also vertically. The entire bottom half of a pattern may be repeated on the top half of the garment in the same or differing colours. It may be repeated identically every four rows or even every two rows. Very advanced players, particularly the type addicted to Multiple Bridge Fairisle, tend to prefer great distances between vertical repeats or even sneaky combinations of apparent repeats that are merely borders for further elaborate work. Repeating the essence of the design but subtly altering the colours used

within an overall plan can make for fascinating reading.

As a rainy day activity, when all the cryptic crosswords have been completed and the chocolate box is still full, try experimenting. Take a sheet of graph paper, mark an arbitrary jersey shape and grab a bunch of coloured pencils. Colour away and enjoy yourself. The non-mathematicians among us may like to begin with the middle two squares so that regardless of where the pattern repeat meets the edges, both left and right sides will at least finish identically. Neutral plain areas at the edges are forgivable and tend to go unnoticed in a completed garment, except by good friends and judges.

A further suggestion for non-mathematicians when experimenting with graphs is to choose a repeat number that ends with zero. This means that you can at least play with triangles with a base of five as well as squares with a base of 10. Total numbers that are divisible by four, five and 10 are ideal — that is, 20, 40, 80, 120, 160 and 200 stitches.

Here's another idea. Choose a small stitch number for your Fairisle (say 40) and enjoy playing with pattern multiples over a small area. In this way you will avoid the problems of running out of yarn, undoing long rows if the pattern doesn't work and possibly making the whole garment the wrong size. Treat the Fairisle piece as a centre panel and later knit two plain side panels to make up the necessary size. An advantage of this method is that the sides of the garment will be stretchy even if the middle panel is not. Most importantly, your Fairisle will have centre-stage presentation, just as it should.

CHOOSING YARN AND COLOURS

Yarn Crepes and worsted yarns are probably the best fibres for Fairisle because they are strong and smooth. After two years of Fairisling one garment (a common occurrence!) you will not want one fine thread to break at the first fence in your path. As a rule, Fairisle is the choice of formal fanatics who prefer a garment to be finished when it is finished, not an ongoing affair.

Crepe or worsted yarn is smooth and slides easily while being worked, which is an asset during the constant twining of yarn at the back of Fairisle knitting. However, do not feel pressured into using these yarns. Textured yarns and even a combination of different weights of yarn can make for a joyful jersey, if so planned.

Colour There are ranges of yarn specifically manufactured for Fairisle work: they include many different tones of one colour and many different colours that are all tonally matched. These are ideal for both traditional and inventive Fairisle.

By using a range of tones within one colour — for instance, light blue, mid blue and dark blue — it is possible to create a subtle gradation of colour, as in a watercolour painting. In this case, it could be done by knitting two rows of dark blue, two in mid blue, two in light blue and perhaps one in white if the blues were clear, or cream if the blues were earthy or smoky.

If you are unsure of a colour scheme for Fairisle work, read the chapter on colour. Choose one or two major colours and tones that appeal and add highlights. These may be simply lighter and darker versions of the main colours. Alternatively, they may be tonally matched complementary colours, giving a touch more drama.

SPECIAL EFFECTS

The reverse side of Fairisle The back of your knitting may hold delightful surprises. The reverse side of Fairisle, in particular, can be as interesting, if not more so, than the front or official side. Unused yarn carried across the back of the work can result in a build-up of texture and braid-like weaving that would be hard to invent deliberately.

The reverse side of the leopard spots on the tummy of the jersey photographed here looked like calligraphy, and the effect was used later in the design as the right side of one shoulder and sleeve. When I began this jersey I hadn't planned it this way, but it turned out better than my original design. The textured effect belonged on the jersey because it was part of its construction. In this garment, combinations of the Fairisle technique (the spots), intarsia (the rainbow effect) and texture (reversed Fairisle calligraphy) resulted in an interesting design that was always entertaining to knit. The knitting became more than simply assembling the appropriate piles of yarn into a wearable garment; it was part of the act of designing.

Zig-Zag Rainbow jersey designed and knitted by Lee Andersen is a combination of modern Fairisle and intarsia work.

CHAPTER SIX

INTARSIA

I ntarsia work has a different basis from Fairisle and textured knitting. Drama and simplicity are the keynotes, often (but not always) provided by striking colour. The garment is usually worked in stocking stitch, row by row, but the different coloured yarns are not carried across the whole width of the work, as in Fairisle. Instead they are crossed over each other at the point where one colour is stopped and another colour begins.

This technique can raise the problem of tangled yarns. The only solution I can offer is to train bullfrogs to swallow the balls of yarn and hop over each other at the appropriate time.

Regardless of the difficulties of this technique it is one worth learning because of the freedom it provides for the designer. More detailed instructions are outlined in this chapter.

Intarsia work with 20 colours in one row may be a nightmare for some knitters, but a challenge to others. In the intarsia work illustrated on the contents page (called "Left-handed Garden") a considerable number of yarns were attached, but the majority were short pieces. When they got into too much of a tangle, I cut them off and changed colour. That was part of the fun.

INTRODUCING NEW COLOURS IN MID ROW

Knit along to the site of the first colour change. Knit the first stitch of the new colour, leaving a 10 cm (4 in.) tail. If you carried on knitting with the new yarn, leaving behind the old one, a little hole would form at the meeting point of the two colours. It will not unravel, so you may like to use it as part of the design. If not, after knitting the first stitch in the new colour, cross the old yarn over the top of the new one, as shown. Then carry on knitting with the new colour. If you wish, the tail can be woven in along the back as you knit to avoid darning it in later. If you weave the tail along a much lighter- or

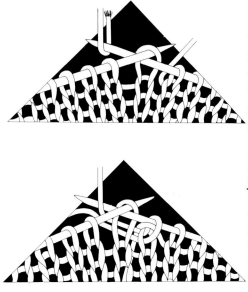

darker-coloured area of the knitting, it will show through, but when it is woven into an area of the same colour it will be practically invisible.

Knotting the new colour to the old one, as well as weaving in the tail, makes for a strong garment, but with fine yarn the knot may show through. The decision is yours. On the return row, at the changeover point, put the right needle tip through the stitch, cross the yarns over each other and then complete knitting the stitch with the correct colour.

As many colours as you like may be introduced in one row.

CROSSING COLOURS ON A VERTICAL LINE

When a colour change creates a vertical division of colour on part of the garment, the twisting of the two yarns takes place between the two colours, after the first row. This will show up on the back of the knitting as something resembling a row of garter stitch on its side.

It is not a great disaster if you neglect to cross the yarns. A small hole will form but, as I said earlier, it will not go anywhere. If you forget again on the next row, the hole will enlarge to form a slit. If this is continued for long enough you will make wonderful slits which may be thonged together later as part of the design, or which may have free-form cables growing out of them, or little hands or faces peeping out. Ms Takes taught me this. I realise some people will not like little hands poking out of their jerseys! Therefore, if you discover a hole in the changeover line between colours, take out your trusty wool needle, the one with the round tip, and sew it up. All fixed!

CROSSING COLOURS ON A DIAGONAL LINE

The same principle as that used with vertical lines applies when working with diagonal colour changes. Diagonals are, in fact, more forgiving, even when you forget to cross over the yarns. Because the line moves every row over one or two stitches, the knitting will hold itself together anyway. (Making slits on a diagonal line involves actually increasing and decreasing stitches.) When working a diagonal colour change it is not necessary to cross the yarns in the same direction every time. If your yarns become twisted in one row it may be possible to untwist them on the next row.

There are two main methods of making diagonal colour changes in intarsia work, and an almost infinite number of variations of these methods.

The first method involves shifting the meeting point of the two colours x number of stitches in each row. This is used for making shallow angles (45 degrees or less) that head off towards the side of the knitting. The second method involves shifting the meeting point one stitch every x number of rows. This method is used when you require the diagonal line to head towards the shoulder (that is, on an angle between 45 and 90 degrees).

Generally, an angle formed by moving one stitch per row and begun on the left hip will end up somewhere around the right underarm area. An angle formed by moving one stitch every two rows and begun on the left hip will generally end up somewhere around the right shoulder. The latter makes an interesting tractor-tyre effect and the yarns tend to untangle themselves more easily.

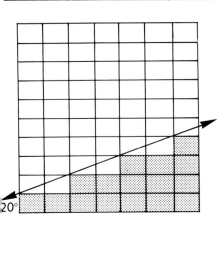

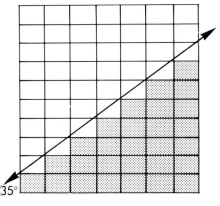

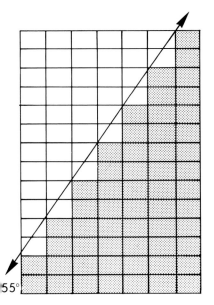

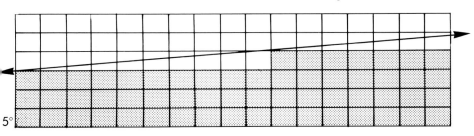

PLANNED DIAGONALS

First knit a swatch so you can work out stitch numbers and rows for the whole garment (see Chapter 4, Measuring and mechanics). Graphing your design on a grid of known stitch and row numbers will give you a good indication of how many stitches per row the line will need to be moved to end up where you want it.

If you have 80 stitches and you wish to make a diagonal line that will cross from one side to the other in exactly 80 rows, you will need to move the colour change one stitch every row, or make little steps by moving the colour change two stitches on the front-facing rows and none on the purl rows. If you have 80 stitches and wish to make a diagonal that will cross from one side to the other in exactly 8 rows, you will need to move the colour changes 10 stitches every row.

This raises a wee difficulty: if the new colour begins 10 stitches earlier on the return purl row, how do you get the yarn to that point without breaking it off and starting again or having a great big loop? The official solution is to plan ahead and weave forward for 10 stitches while knitting the previous plain row. If you forget to do this in anticipation, so to speak, it *is* possible to get the yarn where you want it with just the smallest amount of intelligent cheating.

Assume you are knitting the purl row and have just discovered that you need blue,

but it is waiting 10 stitches away where you left it on the previous plain row. Simply loop it towards you, allowing a lot of slack, cross the old yarn over it as usual and purl the blue stitch normally. Purl a few more stitches, then use the slack blue loop for purling the next stitch. This has the effect of securing the loop into your knitting.

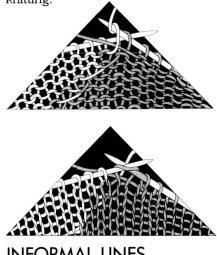

INFORMAL LINES

If diagonal colour changes are consistent over a certain number of stitches and rows, the result will be a straight-lined diagonal. Of course, it is not necessary to be consistent — with planned inconsistency you can make wonderful wiggly lines! Once you are into wiggly-line making, you can start drawing with knitting. Lines that show *action* can be knitted. By definition, there are no instructions on how to do this — you're the artist!

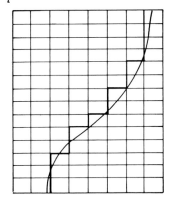

INTARSIA

Top Left: The grey diagonal is a formal background to the blue star shapes and random spaced squares in this jersey by Lynn Williams. **Top Right:** Jan MacDonald's diagonals in hand-dyed mohair. **Below:** Jacket designed by Lee Andersen knitted by Kris Francis showing the intarsia technique, active line and a felted collar. **Inset:** Inside of jacket showing the intarsia technique.

USING A CARTOON

A cartoon is a life-sized plan of the work, used by tapestry weavers as well as knitters. A life-sized paper pattern of the garment is made, and the intarsia design is drawn onto it, providing a guide to progress while the knitting is under way. A good basic cartoon outline can be traced from a sewing pattern for stretch fabric. Stretch patterns are also a good source of ideas for unusual sleeve shapings and constructions.

Use the garment ouline as a colouring-book picture. Cartoons are ideal if you have exact blocks of colour in mind. If the coloured areas are complicated, a cartoon is a

great asset.

While knitting, lay your work upon the cartoon and check progress every now and again. It is easiest to do this in the middle of a row when the stitches are spread evenly over two needles. This brings us to the only major difficulty in working with a full-sized cartoon. Lying down the work to check progress while on public transport is likely to create hostility or unwarranted attention! It is even more difficult to do in smaller family

cars. Those of us who knit on the run may have to avoid knitting from full-sized cartoons when out of the house! A scale drawing (a smaller, less precise version of the cartoon) can be more manageable and perfectly adequate to use as a guide if the garment shaping is simple and familiar.

A cartoon is merely a guide. Don't let it rule once you have drawn it. Two extra spots and one less wiggle in the garment won't worry anyone else, so why should it worry you?

Development of a Diagonal as photographed by Kerry Brown for *More*.
Left: Cartoon with the beginning stage of knitting laid over it.

CALCULATING YARN QUANTITIES

Tangles seem to go hand in hand with intarsia — unless you deviously avoid this fate by working out in advance how much yarn is needed for small blocks of colour or shapes and wind up small amounts of yarn especially for the purpose. (See the section on making yarn dollies in Chapter 3, Yarns.)

To work out the amount of yarn required for a whole row, stretch the stitches across a row and lay the yarn across *three* times to see how much is required for one row. Lay it across *four* times for a casting-off row. Of course, this scientifically devised method of chopping off excess yarn to avoid tangles is laughed and guffawed at by Mr Murphy. He has Murphy's Law on his side, which has a habit of making we knitters run out of yarn two stitches from the end. If we don't there's usually a knot in the yarn anyway.

Another little hint that often doesn't work, though it should, is the "Tie-a-knot-half-way" method of working out whether there is enough yarn left over to finish a piece of knitting. When you are getting close to the end of the ball, fold the remaining yarn in half and tie a knot at the half-way point. Knit the next row. If you have reached the knot already, there is insufficient yarn for another complete row. Even when you haven't reached the knot and are beginning one more row with confidence, Murphy's Law has a habit of stepping in again and thwarting things. This is probably because we forgot to allow some extra yarn for the tail.

Those among us who prefer to apply a different kind of logic will equate this experience with running out of petrol a block before a petrol station. Naturally, we think we must drive faster to get there in time before we run out of fuel. Just as this is idiot logic, so is the desire to knit faster in order to use less yarn before reaching the end of the row; however, I still find myself doing it!

MATCHING SIDES

A major design consideration when working with the human form is the three-dimensional mobile model. All garments intended for everyday wear will be seen front on and side on. Seams are another opportunity to bring together different elements and create an interesting area of interaction.

Designs requiring the intarsia technique are the most likely to have simple clear lines meeting at seams. These lines may match exactly at a seam then go on to do different things on the front and the back. Fronts and backs may be inverse versions of the same image. A diagonal on the front meeting at the side may appear as a chevron design when viewed from the side.

Fronts and backs do not necessarily have to be the same or reversed versions of each other. A line that wiggles on the front may become jagged on the back after crossing the side seam. The seam line then becomes a point of licence to change.

Any lines that do not complete the journey from one edge to the other may do whatever they like within the confines of the garment.

A garment with no relationship at all between front and back makes its own statement about the designer, probably "schizophrenic". No decision at all about the interaction of the front and back seams and shoulder seams indicates just that!

If the garment is random blocks of colour with straight vertical and horizontal lines, the random meeting of colours at the seams is probably quite interesting for the sewer-upper. On the other hand, designs may appear to be mismatched at the sides.

If the front and back designs are complex, for example two paintings, matching them at the sides is almost impossible and probably inadvisable. An alternative is to top and tail the paintings with a black or coloured line and to have a line of the same colour up the side seams. Knitters who design on the needles and never do the front and back the same may choose this border method to overcome the problem of matching the sides.

POCKETS

Pockets do not necessarily have to be square or rectangular. They may be circular, random shaped, kite shaped with flaps, or any shape your hand can fit into. If your intarsia design incorporates dramatic triangular forms, triangular pockets would be a sympathetic choice. Tops higher than the side seams of pockets tend to flop over — but spikey points falling like petals may be the feature of your design.

CASTING ON

Intarsia body design does not have to stop at the bands. Rosemary Mortimer's collage on page 28 required a bottom band that was white on one side and black on the other. It was good design to continue the body division straight on through the band to keep the eye moving up and down, not horizontally. The casting on row was in black and white.

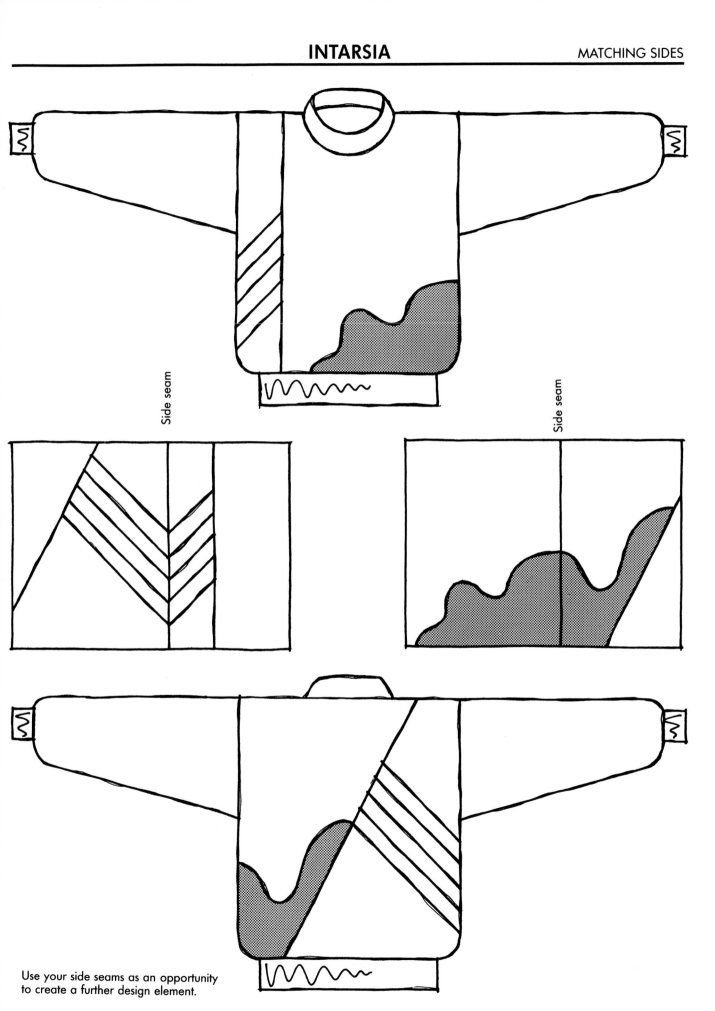

Side seam

Side seam

Use your side seams as an opportunity
to create a further design element.

Bands are often under pressure but there is nothing to stop you from doing them in intarsia — except habit. Leave a long tail when introducing the second (or third or fourth) yarn in the casting on row, and use this to sew the meeting point of two colours firmly together afterwards if you have any worries about your weaving-in technique. Knot the yarns together as well, if you like.

Avoid weaving in along a different colour. Wait until the next row and weave the tail back along the matching colour on every knit stitch. Fairisle bands with a deliberately pulled look creating accordion bumps can be effective, too. Cuffs knitted like this may need buttons because there will be little elasticity.

Right: Two colours pulled tight create a dramatic accordian effect.
Below: Intarsia coat by Lee Anderson, knitted by Rita Riddell.

CASTING OFF

Casting off intarsia work is no different to normal casting off (whatever method you prefer) except the appropriate coloured yarn is used. One hint I've found most valuable for a neat finish is to knit the stitch immediately prior to the colour change in the anticipated colour. When the stitch is slipped over the top it sits over the next colour block and consequently "belongs". If you cast off in exactly the same colour as the stitch in the row below, the result is a slightly staggered appearance.

CHAPTER SEVEN
FINISHING

Most knitters overwhelmingly dislike sewing up their garments. Many people always have a piece of knitting in progress, but never actually get around to putting the pieces together. Their secret is belied by the evidence of piles of knitted sleeves, fronts and backs lurking under cushions or in store cupboards. Their needles are always conveniently misplaced.

By spending a little extra time and effort at the sewing up stage, you will be rewarded many times over. Once you have learnt to sew up correctly, the skill will be yours for life and one you will never regret attaining. It is a rare skill, yet not difficult to learn.

For most of us, the greatest difference between knitting and sewing up is that we have to concentrate and watch what we are doing while sewing up, therefore we put it off or rush the process. If you have put a lot of personal effort and decision making into your garment and it is an original,

unique piece of work, it deserves to be sewn up well. I appeal to your sense of justice on behalf of all unique knitted garments around the world!

There *are* ways of motivating yourself to sew up the pieces of your beautiful unique knit. Vow to become super-good at it, or set yourself a timetable for the whole garment, involving three equal steps of time for planning, knitting and sewing up. Allocate 50 hours to each step, then you can feel marvellous when the sewing up is completed after only five hours! Promise yourself an indulgence (a whole bar of chocolate!) when the task is completed. If the end seems too far away, promise yourself a treat at the end of each section of the sewing up. If all this fails to motivate you, take up knitting on circular needles so your garments don't have seams! Many wonderful books have been written describing this technique, but this isn't one of them. Elizabeth Zimmerman's books are a good starting point.

PRESSING AND BLOCKING

Blocking is another word for the shaping and smoothing of a garment before it is sewn up.

Formal garments can, in some cases, be given a professional look by being blocked and pressed. If stripes are not sitting straight, or if the edges of the knitting are curling, a light press can help. However, before bringing out the iron, check the information on the yarn ball band. Garments made from 100 per cent acrylic will stretch permanently out of shape once pressed that way — and they make terrible dusting rags!

Garments made from textured yarns in informal combinations of techniques may be best sewn up and worn the same day, without blocking and pressing (a flattened piece of handknitting is a piece of knitting with an identity crisis!). Its creation via hundreds or thousands of individual stitches is an essential part of its nature, and reducing it to a flat fabric belies those hours of work. If each little stitch wants to make a statement of individuality, so be it. Pressing and blocking of textured garments is really only an emergency measure, to be used if the garments need to be a little wider or longer. Avoid pressing embossed work and ribbing because its elasticity and texture may be endangered.

If you still wish to press and block your unique knit, cover a table or ironing board with a folded blanket then a sheet. Using rustless pins, block the pieces wrong side out, to the exact measurements required. Any stretching or distortion will become relatively permanent after pressing, so be very careful about deliberately altering the shapes of the pieces. Garment pieces are usually blocked when dry and pressed under a damp cloth. For wool, use a warm, not hot, iron over a damp cloth. The pieces are not actually meant to be ironed, so avoid moving the iron around on the knitting. Lay it down briefly, then lift it again.

Remove the pins while the piece is still damp if you have any doubts about its shape, otherwise let it remain pinned until it is cool and dry.

To help reshape parts of a highly styled garment, such as a puffed sleeve top, stuff the area with crushed, acid-free tissue paper while the garment is drying.

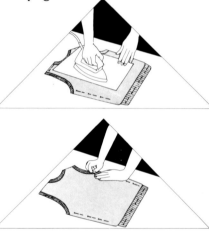

Order of sewing up If you are working from a commercial pattern and want the garment to turn out as shown, follow the instructions for sewing up. The steps involved are usually given in a certain order for sound reasons. Normally, if stitches are to be picked up on double-pointed needles to make a crew or polo neck, the shoulder seams are joined first. If the neckband is to be knitted on ordinary needles, only one shoulder is sewn up before the neck is finished.

Remember that careful matching of stripes on the sides and sleeves helps to achieve a professional finish.

Needles for sewing up Wool or yarn needles especially designed for sewing knitting are available. They have large eyes and are made of metal or plastic. Most importantly, they have rounded tips to help the needle slip between stitches without splitting the yarn and weakening it.

Yarns for sewing up It is probably best to avoid using a heavily textured yarn for assembling a garment because dire frustration can result. Such yarns usually can't be pulled through the stitches. Untwisted yarns, known as roving yarn, tend to be too weak and break at inopportune moments.

The best choice is a smooth, strong yarn that is the same colour or as close as possible to that used in the garment. If the garment includes intarsia work or Fairisle, a number of different yarns may be required in the sewing up. Match the colour of the sewing up yarn with the colour of the knitting at the edges. Alternatively, while the knitting is in progress, deliberately leave long tails of yarn where each new colour is joined in and you will have sewing up yarn just where it is needed.

SEWING UP METHODS

Sewing up methods go by various names, which can make for very confused conversations. A wide range of seams is given because the use of three or four methods, depending on the knitting being sewn up, can lend a garment a professional finish. If the garment includes intarsia work you may be well advised to use various different coloured yarns as well as several different sewing up methods.

Wrong-side-facing, ridged seam (also known as backstitch seam) Backstitch is the most common form of sewing up, particularly on garments that require strong, non-stretch seams. The difficulty with this method is that it is done from the reverse side, making it frustrating to match stripes and shapes. Another problem is that this type of seam forms a ridge. This is not a problem on loose-fitting garments and it can actually be advantageous when used for the shoulders of set-in sleeves which requires the padded shoulders look.

Method: The pieces to be joined are placed together with the right sides facing each other and with the pattern matching row for row and stitch for stitch. Work a backstitch, as in embroidery, along the seam, sewing into the centre of each stitch to correspond with the stitch on the opposite piece. On side seams sew one complete stitch in from the edge. Sew immediately below the cast-off stitch on shoulder seams. One backstitch is worked over every row or over every knitted stitch.

Right-side-facing, flat seam for garter stitch (also known as edge-to-edge seam). This method of sewing up is ideal for garter stitch knitting and other knitting with little knobs along the side edges. Stocking stitch with a slip stitch edge also has pips or little knobs that can be sewn with this method for a lacy, decorative seam. (To make a slip stitch edge, slip the first stitch of each row knitwise then knit the last stitch of each row. The first stitch of the purl row is slipped knitwise.) This sewing-up method is most useful for lightweight knits. Used on garter stitch, it is almost invisible.

Method: Place the pieces to be joined edge to edge, front side facing, with the little knobs

of the knit stitches locking together. Sew into the knob of each alternate stitch. The sewing yarn may be pulled tight to wedge the alternate knobs into each other, or it may be left loose, forming a part stitch between the pieces of knitting. The sewing yarn will always show, so it is necessary to match it well or use the same yarn as that used in the knitting.

Right-side-facing, flat figure-of-eight seam This method of sewing up is suited to joining two pieces that have been knitted in different directions (for instance, knitting on an angle. See sewing in sleeves). In fact, it was devised especially for that purpose. It is ideal for setting off-the-shoulder sleeves into armholes.

Method: With the right side

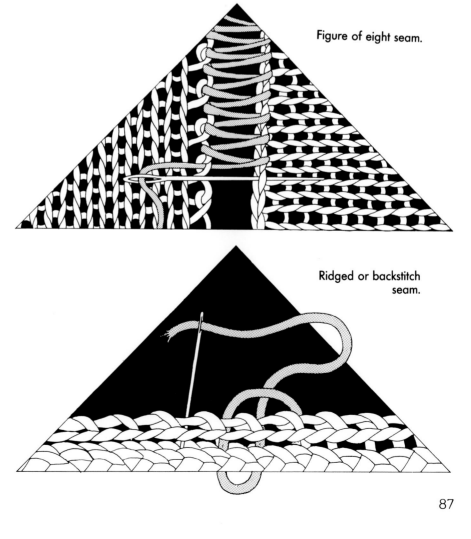

Flat seam for garter stitch.

Figure of eight seam.

Ridged or backstitch seam.

facing, join the sewing yarn to the edge of the piece. Pass the needle under and up through the edge of the other piece of knitting. Take it down through the gap between the two pieces of work, then up through the edge of the first piece. Now take it down through the gap between the two pieces of knitting again. Continue making figure-of-eight stitches in this manner.

If one edge is made up of the top ends of stitches (for example, a sleeve top) and the other edge is made up of row sides (for example, the armhole of the body piece of the garment), the stitches will not match one for one with the rows, but this is not a problem with this method.

Right-side-facing, half-ridge invisible bar seam (also known as running-stitch seam, ladder-stitch seam, bar-stitch seam). This method is ideal for most seams and is worked from the right side, so matching stripes and patterns is easier. The stitch duplicates stocking stitch, so that across the seam the pattern of the stitches continues without interruption.

Method: With the right sides facing and the edges aligned, insert the needle from the wrong side to the right side between the first and second

rows. Cross to the other piece of knitting and insert the needle between the first and second rows, then out between the second and third rows, picking up two cross threads or bars. Return to the first side, insert the needle where the yarn comes from and pick up two cross threads or bars as before. Continue in this way, leaving the sewing thread stitches about 1 cm (⅜ in.) long, until about 2 cm (¾ in.) has been worked, then pull the thread tightly enough to close the seam without the sewing yarn showing. It is a good idea to use a matching yarn to sew with because it will show when the garment seam is under stress.

A development on this sewing-up method is to insert the needle back in under the next bar up the seam instead of where the yarn comes out. This makes for a more open seam which may be quite sufficient for lightweight, looser garments.

SEWING UP ON A MACHINE

Many machine knitters sew up their garments on a sewing machine. Handknits can also be sewn up on a machine. Machine sewing of seams with the wrong sides together can provide an informal look to an otherwise structured design. If

the seam is in the front, the "inside-out" look is accentuated.

A straight stitch rather than a zig zag stitch is usually best for machined seams as a zig zag stitch tends to push out the seam into waves. Some machines have a stretch stitch, which is ideal for sewing handknits. A polyester cotton mix thread is suitable for most machine sewn seams.

Basting can save hours of frustration.

Textured yarns may be easier to sew if a sheet or strip of tissue paper is placed over the knitting but under the machine foot. The paper is sewn through, then torn off afterwards. This stops things like mohair and lumps of novelty yarns getting caught in the foot. If the yarn is particularly unruly, a further layer over the feed dog and under the knitting will also help.

TO SEW UP OR NOT TO SEW UP

Not sewing up can be even better than sewing up garments, on occasion. By leaving regular or irregular gaps in the seam along the outside edge of a batwing sleeve line, you can provide interest in an otherwise ordinary garment. The connection points can be made into the focal point of the garment by the ingenious use of fastenings — unique buttons or leather ties, tiny pearl buttons or metal clips . . . anything you like.

Edges Any edge of a garment can be decorated or used as a feature of the garment. Fine, lacy crochet edges; rolls that have been bound with a contrasting thread, lace, ribbon; drawstrings . . . the possibilities are only as limited as you want to make them.

Bar-stitch seam.

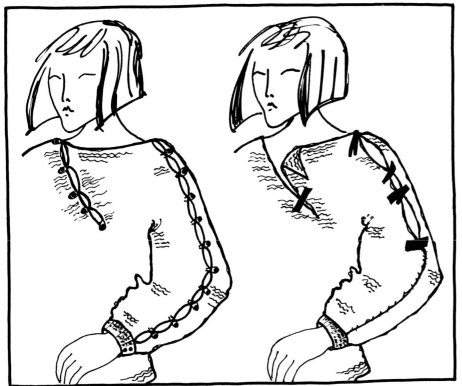

SETTING IN SLEEVES

A garment that is too tight under the arms is one of the most uncomfortable things to wear. Remember that jerseys are generally worn over the top of other garments, and allow plenty of room for movement in this area.

Mark the centre point of the top of the sleeve, and pin or baste it in place at the shoulder seam. Ease in the sleeve on either side of the shoulder seam. It is a good idea to baste in the sleeves and try on the garment before doing the final sewing, particularly if the sleeve has gathers or something unusual about it.

For a boat-necked garment
Boat- or slash-neck garments can be more comfortable to wear if the back is about 3 cm (1 in.) longer than the front. This means that the shoulder seams will lie forward of the shoulder, but the sleeves can be set in normally, with the centre of the sleeve top being at the centre of the wearer's shoulder.

Baste together the under armhole and sleeve seams, then lay the garment out flat. The shoulder line will naturally come forward, and the centre of the sleeve top will naturally fold in half and find it's correct place to join at the shoulders. This point will be slightly behind the shoulder seam.

Setting in sleeves for off-the-shoulder styles The two most important points to note with this style are the depth of the sleeve hole and the need to stretch rather than ease in the sleeve. An off-the-shoulder sleeve for the average female measures about 20 cm (8 in.) deep, or 40 cm (16 in.) in circumference. For a large male, the sleeve opening may measure approximately 30 cm (12 in.) deep and 60 cm (24 in.) in circumference.

An off-the-shoulder sleeve must be cast off loosely. If it is not, the sleeve will puff out when it is set in, particularly around the top of the shoulder. This may do nice things for the biceps of some people, but not

Make the back larger than the front on a boat- or slash-necked garment.

for the rest of us. However, it is relatively easy to remedy. If necessary, undo the last few rows of the sleeve and cast off again loosely. You will need to lose one row in the process, because extra yarn will be required to cast off loosely. Now undo the side seam until the armhole is deep enough. Set in the sleeve again, watching the area around the

shoulder seam in particular. The sleeve will not match stitch for stitch with the armhole, but this doesn't matter.

The ladder or figure-of-eight sewing up methods are best for this area of the garment especially, because it is a flat seam and does not make a hard ridge under the arm.

To pull in droopy shoulders or reinforce the shoulders of

heavy garments, stitch a piece of seam tape to the insides of the shoulder seams. Off-the-shoulder-styles are *supposed* to drop, but if after a few washes you find the sleeves are getting too long and the shoulder area seems to be stretching, use seam tape to remedy the problem quickly.

Cut up jerseys sewn with embellishments create a dramatic full-length male coat.

TC

CHAPTER EIGHT

EMBELLISHMENTS

J ust as entertaining the eye can enhance a meal, the addition of decorative touches to garments can affect the way they make the wearer feel. However, not every piece needs embellishment; some are wonderful the moment they are worn on the human form.

The majority of decorative additions to knitting fall into five categories:
° Embroidery and Swiss darning.
° Knitted and crocheted additions.
° Natural objects.
° Manufactured objects.
° Felted additions.

EMBROIDERY AND SWISS DARNING

Entire books have been written on embroidery, and almost every type of embroidery stitch may be applied to knitting if a few basic traps are avoided. The elasticity of the knitting must be maintained, so work the embroidery loosely over tightly stretched knitting. Use a wool needle with a blunt tip to avoid splitting the yarn and weakening the knitting. Some appropriate stitches to use are satin stitch over small areas, chain stitch, back stitch, stem stitch, French knots and cross stitch.

Embroidery can be used deliberately to pull an area of a garment into a tighter weave. It can be used on the shoulders or yoke to create a blouson effect over the bust. It is ideal also for adding a textured look to a flat area and for adding eyes and tiny details that look awkward if knitted.

Swiss darning, or duplicate stitch, or knitting stitch, is an embroidery stitch formed by

Embroidered seams.

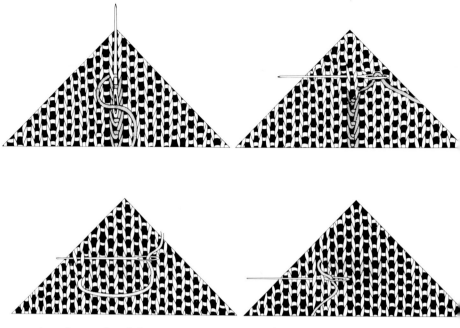

retracing the path of the original stitch, thereby covering it. It can be used to create the look of Fairisle or colour work patterns on a stocking stitch background. It is ideal also for use where it is inconvenient to knit in a small area of colour and for fine lettering and small decorations.

A disadvantage of Swiss darning is that it doubles the thickness of the knitted stitch and can, therefore, result in

weight-distribution problems if used over a wide area.

Swiss darning is useful for the correction of errors in Fairisle work. It is also handy if a curve needs "improving" in intarsia work. The whole V shape of the stitch does not need to be completed. Careful embroidering of just one half of it can disguise a skip in a two-row diagonal, for instance, so that even you won't be able to relocate it.

KNITTED AND CROCHETED ADDITIONS

Knitted additions include motifs, bobbles added

afterwards in a variety of colours, fringes and French knitted tubes winding their way through the knitting or just hanging off at random points. These are only a few of the many possibilities.

Further information on knitted embellishments may be found in Chapter 4 (Measuring and mechanics).

Motifs The addition of separate shapes to a garment can add interest and delight youngsters (and oldsters). They can be as simple as a balloon that has been padded with dacron or as complex as a little person, complete with separate trousers, braces and hat. Motifs do not need to be completely sewn down. A hole at the top of a basket (perhaps knitted in basket stitch) may have room for the small owner's fingers and actually serve as a pocket.

NATURAL OBJECTS

All sorts of natural objects may be added to a garment to enhance both day and evening wear. Try plant seeds, metal, bone, feathers and stones with holes drilled in them (why not diamonds, if you're eccentric — and rich!). If the object is not washable, try gluing or sewing it to a brooch back so that it may be easily removed and replaced. Use earring hooks so that delightful goodies may be incorporated in a garment one day and worn in the ear the next. Versatility is the key!

Natural additions would obviously suit a garment made from natural-coloured yarns, enhancing the earthy feel of the piece. Plain or coloured wooden beads are wonderful for this purpose. Even a set of small wooden beads tucked into the centres of a row of cables would personalise a garment.

Natural wools in the cream, brown and browny-grey range are enhanced by gold-red beads. A set of purply-red beads would look happier on natural yarns in tones of black, grey, charcoal and pure white.

Why not follow through the natural animal fibre theme by incorporating leather or sheepskin additions? Thonging is strong and relatively stable, whereas strips of leather and suede are softer and less stable (in other words, they can stretch). Knitted leather strips incorporated in a limited stress area of the knitting work well. Alternatively, try sewing or threading on with thonging leather patches of any shape or size.

Sheepskin addition to a neckline.

Lyre-Bird suede neckline.

Sequins There are two main types of sequins: metal-based discs in silver, gold and other metallic colours; plastic-based discs in every colour imaginable. Some sequins are not designed to be washed and their colours may run, or they may even melt. Check them by washing a few first if they are not packaged with special instructions.

Sequins are usually sewn onto a garment by passing a thread through the centre hole, across the outside of the sequin and back down through the fabric. If you prefer, you can avoid crossing the sequin with the thread by attaching it with a tiny bead positioned over the hole in the sequin. The thread is passed up through the centre of the sequin, through the bead and back down through the sequin. This technique works with any object larger than the sequin hole but not as big as the sequin itself.

MANUFACTURED OBJECTS

Into this category fit all the wonderful inventions of our species that are small enough to attach to the human form while allowing it to remain mobile.

Before deciding which embellishment to use, consider the purpose of the garment, the weight of the addition and the effect that it will have on the knitted fabric and its care and washing requirements.

A leather-yoked jersey incorporating knitted suede strips. The yoke is tied to the knitting by the fringes.

Secondly, have fun.

Look for objects in places like millinery supply stores, flea markets, emporiums, haberdashery counters, hobby craft shops and among your own treasure troves. Some possibilities are ribbons, fabric petals, beads, motifs, lace, seed pearls, sequins, paillettes (large sequins), rhinestones, buttons and embroidery threads.

A sequin-tailed mermaid graces the back of a jacket with sea imagery. It combines knitting, crochet, embroidery and quilting.

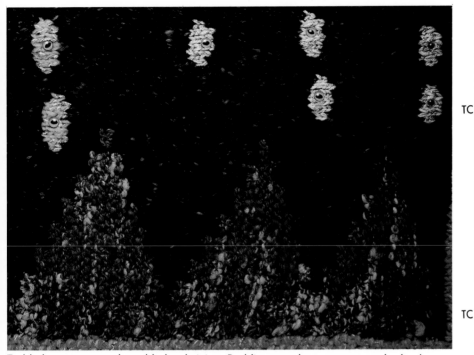

Teddy bear eyes can be added to knitting. Padding may be necessary at the back to cover the shanks.

Buttons If your garment needs buttons and it is a unique knit, why not use handmade buttons of your own creation? Fimo is ideal for this purpose. First soften it by hand

TC

Sliced rolls of Fimo make interesting buttons.

TC

Embroidered buttons by Heather Nicholson.

TC

Jocelyn McGregor knitted this waistcoat sideways, incorporating wooden beads and buttons.

Beads Beads are ideal embellishments for original knits because of their huge variety in shape, size and materials. They may be round, cylindrical, square, disc and pendant shaped and made from glass, wood, metal, bone, crystal, precious and semi-precious stones or plastic. Seek them out in old jewellery boxes as well as from retail outlets. Strings of beads and ready-made beaded appliques are also available.

Beads may be knitted into a garment or added on after completion. If you are knitting beads into the fabric of the work and don't want the knitting to curl, include them in every second row instead of every row. For a neat edge, try leaving the beads off the two or three stitches on each outer edge. For sewing beads onto a garment, extremely fine, long and flexible beading needles are available. Use a strong cotton or silk thread and knot the thread on each side of the bead to prevent it falling between the knitting stitches.

Take care to fasten off the thread securely by stitching over and over at the back.

Prestrung beads may be sewn on to a garment in short lengths to minimise stress and stretching of the thread and the knitting. When stringing beads, use a double thread or special clear nylon beading thread. Alternatively, wax the thread by drawing it through beeswax, or buy prewaxed thread.

Consider the weight of the beaded embellishment at the design stage, if possible, and take steps to minimise stress on the knitting. Beaded appliques may be stabilised by backing the knitting to which they are attached with a fine piece of fabric and stitching through all the layers.

EMBELLISHMENTS

manipulation, then roll, press or slice it into shapes. With a bit of experimentation, you will be able to combine colours to make abstract or picture buttons to suit the knitting. For instance, buttons bearing a spot within a different coloured circle can be made by laying a thin roll of Fimo within a thicker outer roll, like wire within a cable. The design shows up when the Fimo roll is sliced like a jam roll.

After slicing the buttons, make holes in them so they may be sewn on to the knitting, then bake them in the oven at 130°C or 275°F for about 10 to 15 minutes. The buttons will harden upon cooling.

If they are not hard enough after cooking, bake them for a little longer. Further cooking will make the buttons go glassy and the colours become more natural, like pottery glazes. Reds become brick red to brown, and bright grass green becomes soft moss green. Sometimes the Fimo pops, creating barklike effects. Too much cooking will result in black, crumbly buttons resembling charcoal. I know these things!

Toggles Toggles may be made from leather offcuts for fastening garment openings. Cut the leather into tapering strips measuring the anticipated width of the toggle at one end and about a quarter of that width at the other. Cut two slits in the middle to allow the finer end to be threaded through and fastened. Roll up the wide end of the strip to the position of the slits, then wrap the tail

or narrow end around the toggle and through both slits. Pull it tight. Use the tail to attach the toggle to the garment.

Ribbon beading, banding and ruching Ribbons can be used to vary a design in a myriad of ways. Velvet and satin ribbon, lace ribbon, fine braids and leather strips are just a few possibilities.

The weaving or lacing of ribbons through the fabric of a garment is called *ribbon beading*. Holes are usually especially made in the knitting with a lace or eyelet stitch, but it *is* possible to thread ribbons through loosely worked stocking stitch. The weaving may be done horizontally, vertically, diagonally or in curves. The only limiting factor is that the ribbon should be caught into the work at suitably distant intervals to avoid buckling and stretching of the knitting but without leaving loops that may catch on projecting objects.

The ribbon ends may be sewn into seams or rolled and stitched carefully to the edges of the knitting. Try securing them with tiny seed pearls, motifs, lace medallions or decorative knots. Alternatively, leave them free as a feature of the design. They could be used as decorative ties, button loops or fringes. The possibilities are endless.

If you wish to leave the ribbon ends free, prevent fraying by cutting them diagonally, or fold them in half lengthways, then cut on a diagonal towards the fold. A

firm knot, a folded and stitched hem or a flame-sealed edge for nylon ribbon are other options.

Many different types of ribbon are available, but it is a good idea to choose one that requires the same washing and care as the rest of the garment.

Staple weaving is a technique similar to ribbon beading in which staples of clean, unspun fleece are threaded through the work. They may be naturally coloured or oven-dyed with the technique described in the felting section later in this chapter. If the threaded staples are very short, it is probably safer to stitch them gently into place, always allowing for the elasticity of the knitting. Short staples are more likely to stay in place if the knitted background stitches are of pure wool also.

Ribbon banding is the sewing of ribbons or braids on top of the fabric of the garment. Stitch both sides of the ribbon in the same direction to avoid puckering. If, however, you desire a puckered effect, try basting one edge of the ribbon with a running stitch, then pull the thread to gather it before sewing it onto a garment.

Ribbon ruching is the pleating of ribbons onto a knitted background. Either sew a long running stitch on each edge of the ribbon, with the stitches exactly in line, and pull the two threads evenly to form pleats; or, sew one line of running stitch along the centre of the ribbon, pull to pleat the ribbon and sew down the pleats by backstitching along the centre of the ribbon.

Both gathering and ruching are ideal for forming curved lines with ribbon. With all these techniques it is essential to allow for the elasticity of the knitted background to avoid strain and breaking of the ribbon or decorative thread.

FELTING

The intention of this section of the book is to describe how to cause felting of wool, which may seem strange when people have been known to go to great lengths to avoid the

felting of finished woollen garments. Felting is what takes place when the wool fibres become sufficiently entangled to form a solid fabric, usually as a result of the wrong treatment of a jersey. Most of us will know the frustration of

Pale blue felted neck frill on a handspun fringed jersey.

Above: Striving for Success with a detachable felted collar.
Below: Felted neck frill on a handspun wool jacket.

TC

taking a woollen garment out of the wash and finding it shrunk and felted into an inflexible mass. Felting occurs as a result of excessive handling of wool while wet (especially by inanimate objects like washing machines) and transferring it too quickly from hot to cold water.

Despite these negative aspects, felting can be used to great advantage to form collars and other decorative embellishments for knitting. The felted fabric may be cut or beaten into a body-fitting curve. As a fabric for complete items of clothing, however, felting has limitations. It tends to pill when rubbed excessively and it sags or accommodates weight and pressure without reverting to its previous shape when the pressure is removed, as knitting does.

Felting has a long tradition in some countries. In the past it was usually done with naturally coloured wool, but there is no reason why chemically dyed or naturally dyed fleece cannot be used. Most dyeing methods are suitable for colouring fleece before felting, but it is also possible to dye it afterwards. Depending on the results you require, fleece dyeing may take place in the oven or on the stove or by natural sunlight (solar dyeing). Because it is harsh on the fibres, like the felting process itself, oven dyeing is well suited to felting. (However, it does strip the wool of its natural oils and you may therefore want to add oil should you wish to spin the fleece after dyeing it in this way.)

Oven dyeing of fleece This technique provides multi-coloured staples in one dyeing session. It is very similar to cooking a roast (sometimes I find the end products hard to

distinguish, but cooking has never been my forte!).

Method: Fill a large roasting dish with sheep fleece. Fill the dish with water. Salt to taste or add vinegar (to fix the dye) and sprinkle on the dye powder. Bake for one hour at 180°C (350°F).

As you can see, there's very little to this process. The key elements are not to prod and poke the wool too much and to use more than one dye colour. One tin of red dye sprinkled in one corner of the dish, and another of blue in the opposite corner and yellow in another (take your pick) will result in an intermingling rainbow of colours. Try not to allow too much intermixing of colours unless you require brown, brown and more brown.

Suitable dyes for this techique are Dylon hot-water powdered dyes, Panhue dyes and Ciba dyes. Others may work well, but I haven't tried them. You needn't use a whole tin of each colour, especially strong colours like dark blue, which can easily take over. You can be fairly heavy-handed with a "weak" colour like yellow.

When the dyeing is completed, rinse the fleece thoroughly in warm water. If you plunge it straight into cold water the felting process will begin immediately and you may not be able to separate the staples for carding later, if that is required. Gentle cooling will provide more choice in the final appearance of the felted wool.

Pot dyeing of fleece Colour changes that occur within an individual staple of wool provide attractive and interesting effects. To retain the staple form while dyeing is taking place, put the staples in an onion bag or other

open-weave bag before dyeing. Lower the bag into a pot of boiling water and dyestuff on the stove and let it remain there for 20 to 30 minutes or the time specified on the dye tin. By moving the bag into another dyepot and only partially overdyeing the staples with another colour, you can obtain multi-coloured effects along the length of the staples. Different tones can be obtained by varying the amount of time the bag remains in dyepots of different colours.

Fleece for felting does not have to contain randomly dyed or multicoloured staples, nor do the staples have to be well-formed. In most traditional felting the fleece is carded and all trace of the staples is obliterated. It is up to you to decide which method to use.

The felting process Felted fabric is obtained by placing several different layers of fleece at right-angles to each other, immersing them in water baths of widely differing temperatures and beating them into submission.

In order to control the felting process you will need to take some interceding measures.

First, you'll need a method of holding the fleece in a predetermined position during felting. For small pieces of work, use sheets of netting, tulle or organza. Lay out the material and build up the fleece on top of it. The more layers of fleece, the better it will felt. Four layers is a good number, but vary this according to the amount of strength and thickness required in the end product. The final layer is usually the one that is seen, but by taking care in placing the fleece on the underside you can produce a reversible felted fabric, perhaps of differing colours on the top and bottom.

After rinsing, the fleece may be carded to obtain special effects. The individual staples should still be relatively obvious and capable of being pulled out.

If you require an effect whereby the staples remain intact, card or tease only the cut end of the staple. A carding comb is not necessary for this purpose — your fingers will do. Put a fine layer of well-carded, matching-coloured fleece at right-angles to the cut end of the staples to hold it all together during and after felting.

Further decoration may be added by laying spun wool yarn over the fleece in an appropriate design. Crepe or worsted yarns felt less readily than softly spun or fluffy yarns.

After the design and fleece are laid out, a second sheet of fine fabric is placed over the top and all the layers are stitched together to hold the fleece in place while it receives the rough treatment necessary for felting. An ordinary cotton thread is suitable. Stitch through the layers at intervals close enough to hold the design but not so close that you will have difficulty removing them. Some sewing machines have a suitable basting stitch.

If your design involves leaving the staple tails free at the edges, baste them down, too, to stop them felting to the other staple tails and forming interesting lumps and holes, unless that is the effect your require.

Now you are ready to begin felting. Clear the entire bench (plus the kitchen, house and neighbourhood if you're really going to get stuck in!). Put towels on the floor and remove anything precious from the vicinity. Put a kettle or zip

on to boil. Fill a sink with some cold water and ice cubes if you have them. If you're felting on a large scale, the bathtub would be more suitable. Use the ice packs you keep for camping or hangovers. Fill a large bowl with warm water, squirt some dishwashing liquid onto the intended victim and give it a warm bubble bath. The idea is that the fibres become slippery and morally decadent, entangling themselves in each others' arms!

Remove the fleece from the warm water, lay it on the bench and hit it with a rolling pin, or roll it up in a tight roll and twist it for good measure. When you think it has had enough, pour boiling water over it, hit it again, roll it, twist it and shout at it. Now pour on a little more hot water, which should cause the fleece to fizz and puff up. Hit it a few more times, then plunge it straight into the bath of cold water. The extreme change in temperature causes the fibres to cling to each other with fright. This is, in essence, felting.

Now look at your piece of felting. If frizzy bits of wool are poking out of the netting or fine fabric, it may be ready. If they are poking out and felting together over the top of the netting it is definitely done, and you may have a piece of felting with the netting permanently attached.

The chances are that you will need to put the fleece through three or four of these soapy, hot-cold sessions to obtain any obvious reaction. If you require a lightly felted piece, check on it after one or two sessions. There is no need to dry it between treatments.

You can give the piece a final zap by throwing it into a hot spin dryer. This tends to complete the felting process,

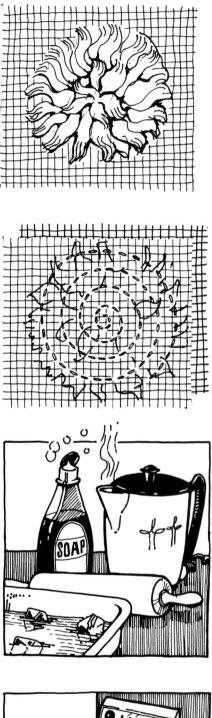

but if you're too enthusiastic it may emerge as a small, puckered, thick blob, ideal for use as material for finger puppets, coasters or slipper soles!

Due to its experience in the school of hard knocks, felted pieces are ideal additions to knitting. They are more forgiving of hard washing than ordinary knitted yarn because they have been there already. However, you may wish to make the felting removable, as in the jersey entitled Striving for Success. It is stitched loosely to the garment around the base of the crew neck and the garment is complete but less exciting without it.

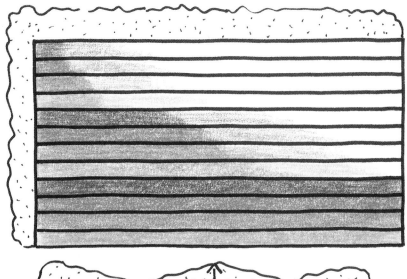

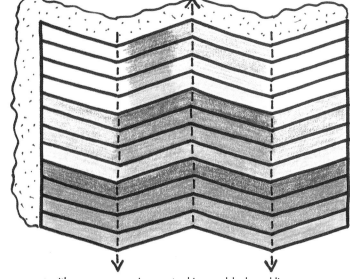

QUILTING AND PADDING

Padding and quilting can create interesting effects, especially if the direction of the sewing is exaggerated. Patching and quilting shoulders, elbows and knees adds strength and interest. Back quilted areas with fine stretch fabric and stuff them with dacron for bulk.

Batwing garment with crosses crossing a stockingpadded neckline.

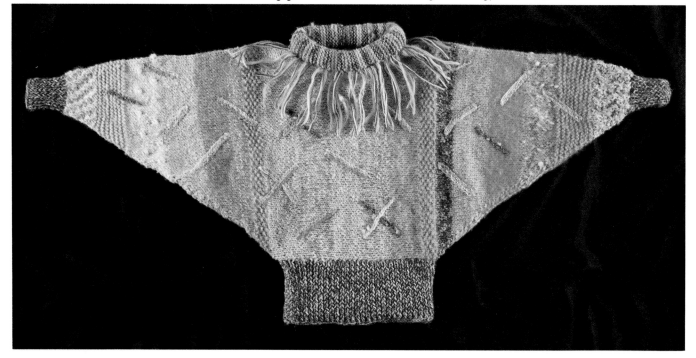

CHAPTER NINE

DISASTERS

Everyone has them . . . but all is not lost. Disasters can be turned to advantage. For most knitting problems there is a cure. The terminal cases can be used as a starting point for a new departure, perhaps inspiring something that otherwise wouldn't have seen the light of day. So take out of the cupboard all those half-finished, boring, wrong-sized, weird-shaped creations.

DISASTERS

STAIN REMOVAL

Alcoholic drinks Apply diluted ammonia to stain and rub well with a damp, lukewarm cloth. (Also see Beer.)

Anti-perspirant Rub a mixture of 10 per cent water, 40 per cent soap and 50 per cent solvent onto the stain. Remove with a damp, lukewarm cloth.

Ballpoint pen Treat with eucalyptus oil or methylated spirits, then squeeze gently in approved wool detergent suds, and rinse thoroughly.

Beer Rinse at once in cold water, then squeeze gently in approved wool detergent suds, followed by a thorough rinse in clean water. Diluted white vinegar may help remove stubborn stains — again rinse thoroughly.

Beetroot Sprinkle with absorbent powder (e.g. salt, talc) and leave overnight before removing. Then apply a weak solution of white vinegar or lemon juice with cold water, followed by an enzyme washing product. NB: Wool products should not be left to soak in enzyme products, as these attack proteins like wool.

Blood Rinse thoroughly in cold water, then soak the stained section in a solution of approved wool detergent suds, following the instructions on the packet. Do not dry until the stain has been removed.

Butter Treat with drycleaning fluid (perchlorethylene), allow to evaporate, rinse the area in cold water, then gently work in approved wool detergent suds, and rinse again.

Cocoa As for butter.

Coffee (black or white) As for butter.

Crayon Treat with drycleaning fluid (perchlorethylene), lighter fuel or mineral turpentine. Caution: Ensure that no flame or lighted cigarette is near and use in a well-ventilated area. Then apply a solution of one teaspoon of approved wool detergent with one litre of warm water.

Cream As for crayon, but in reverse order of treatment.

Egg As for blood.

Fruit and fruit juice If treated immediately, nearly all fruit stains can be removed with cold water and approved wool detergent suds.

Grass Treat with clean methylated spirits.

Gravy and sauces Use drycleaning fluid or eucalyptus oil. Allow to evaporate completely, then work warm, approved wool detergent suds into the stain, and then blot with a clean, damp cloth. Repeat this treatment if necessary, and rinse thoroughly in clean water.

Grease As for gravy.

Ink As for beer.

Lipstick Treat with eucalyptus oil or drycleaning fluid. Allow to evaporate completely, then squeeze gently in approved wool detergent suds and rinse thoroughly.

Mildew Treat with a solution of one teaspoon of approved wool detergent with one litre of warm water, followed by a solution of one part Hydrogen Peroxide (20 vol.) diluted with 10 parts of cold water. Caution:

Do not use on dark or patterned knits.

Milk As for butter.

Mustard As for beer.

Oil As for gravy.

Paint (emulsion) Blot up excess paint immediately, flush with water and pat dry. Repeat process until clean.

Paint (oil based) Apply mineral turpentine or other suitable solvent immediately and blot dry. This process may need to be repeated several times.

Perspiration Rub first with warm water and ammonia and then with diluted lemon juice.

Rust Treat with lemon juice or diluted white vinegar. Rinse thoroughly.

Scorch marks Gently scrape away burnt fibre ends. With white fabric, very diluted Hydrogen Peroxide may then be used. Rinse thoroughly.

Shoe polish Treat with drycleaning fluid or eucalyptus oil, then squeeze gently in approved wool detergent suds, and rinse thoroughly.

Soft drinks As for fruit juice.

Tar As for oil paint.

Tea (black or white) As for butter. Soak stubborn stains in pure glycerine for a short time between treatments.

Wine Dab the stained area with clean paper tissue or absorbent cloth with water containing a little ammonia — or dust liberally with absorbent powder such as chalk or talc. Allow to stand. Shake off and rinse area thoroughly with clean water. Salt assists the removal of red wine stains. Cover the area immediately with a thick layer of salt, and leave for several hours until all the moisture is absorbed.

RESURRECTING SHRUNK GARMENTS

Probably every handknitter has encountered the problem of an over-zealous husband, friend or flatmate who has shrunk one of their creations in the wash. I'm no exception.

To avoid such terrible shocks, hide your dirty washing in a locked cupboard or keep the washing instructions that come with most yarns in a prominent place. If this advice comes too late, try the following methods of giving shrunk garments a new life.

Slightly shrunk Block and press the garment a number of times, hopefully enlarging it each time.

Slight shrinking can actually be an advantage if the garment was slightly stretched. After a number of wearings I throw one of my favourites into the machine for a gentle wash in lukewarm water and a cold rinse which pulls it back into shape. My husband, Paul, who has never hand-washed anything other than himself in his life, "washed" two of my jerseys in the only way he knew — in the machine on its normal cycle. I remarked on how lovely and fluffy and "contained-looking" these garments were before I realised what he had done.

Definitely shrunk Garments which fit this description are to be donated to smaller people in colder climates (preferably people with long arms and short bodies!). If the body part is still comfortable, chop some off the arms to put the garment back into proportion.

Hopeless cases If a garment is shrunk and felted beyond repair, felt it completely (see Chapter 8, Embellishments) after undoing the side seams (if you can). Use the pieces for patches on jeans and other garments, for padded shoulders on sweatshirts, as padding for seat cushions and oven mitts, for making mittens, slippers and hats or for incorporating into wallhangings and rugs.

If you have enough hopeless cases, felt them to a matching thickness, cut them into squares or some other patchwork shape, dye the pieces if necessary to give them co-ordinating colours and sew them together, seam edge outwards, into a giant jacket or blanket. Wonderful!

REDEEMING OVERTIGHT FAIRISLE

Overtight Fairisle can't really be fixed, but it can be altered and made into a feature of a new garment. First gather it further or quilt it on a machine over a padded backing fabric. Turn it sideways and use it as a centre panel on the back or front of a garment, or position it down the middle of the sleeves. Knit the remaining pieces of the garment in a plainer pattern to highlight the gathered Fairisle panels.

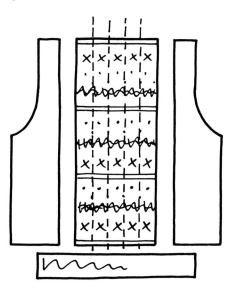

CORRECTING FAIRISLE ERRORS

Refer to the section on Swiss darning in Chapter 8, Embellishments.

MINOR TENSION ERRORS

Loose purl rows are a common problem. Look out for this early in your knitting and, if necessary, use a smaller needle for the purl rows. If you are not bothered by loose purl rows in your knitting, take advantage of them when counting rows. If there is a difference in tension between your knit and purl rows, they will show up as neat pairs on the back of the work.

CHANGING THE COLOUR

If you detest the colour but love the shape of a garment, try dyeing the entire garment. Use chemical or natural dyes. If the piece contains more than one type of yarn, remember that the different yarns will dye differently and even various fibres within a yarn will pick up the dye unevenly, or not at all in the case of synthetic fibres. This phenomenon is actually an advantage in attaining unusual effects. Before choosing a new dye colour, look at the colours of the synthetic fibres in the garment which will probably remain the same. A flecked yarn will be more forgiving of variations in dyeing.

Method: Use a large dye pot, allowing plenty of room for movement and free circulation of dye and water to promote an even effect. Raise the temperature slowly and don't poke and prod the garment too much (rapid changes of temperature and overhandling cause felting). Follow the instructions on the dye container regarding rinsing and timing.

HOLES

So there is a hole in your garment. There are several options.

° Mend it.
° If you have matching yarn, Swiss darn inside the hole. If not, take some matching yarn from the neck if it is a polo neck or from the ribbing if it is of a good length.
° Cut new holes to match the one that is already there. Line them with coloured pieces of machine knitting or stretch fabric and sew around the outside. Alternatively, for a raggy look, leave them to fray.
° Proceed as above, but bind the edge with buttonhole stitch or decorative stretch lace and put a layer of matching silk fabric underneath each hole.
° If the hole appears in an appropriate place, cover it with a motif.
° Embroider a cobweb in the hole and add a spider creeping out from the armpit to flash at inquisitive friends. Or, add a caterpillar and leaf.
° For a really exotic solution embroider on the garment the words, "This is a hole", and add arrows pointing in the appropriate direction.

Embroidered blocks of colour on knitting are an ideal way to cover permanent accidents. A layer of fine fabric stabilises the knitting.

MINOR DISASTERS

Accepting the random element as friend, not foe, requires you to acknowledge any potentially frustrating events and turn them to your advantage. Quite minor problems, such as running out of yarn in the middle of the row, are not grounds for throwing your needles across the room. Such an occurrence merely indicates, according to my lifelong tutor Ms Takes, that it is time to change colours, add a little fringe or rescue dinner.

If you drop a stitch you don't have to rush and locate a crochet hook, loosing the rest of the stitches in the process. A dropped stitch is probably a hint that summer is coming. The lovely lacy effect caused (excuse me — achieved!) by the constant releasing of stitches could be precisely what the garment needs.

Controlling the random element (or pretending that you meant the garment to be how it has turned out) is not impossible. A mistake can be brought into line after the event simply by repeating it elsewhere in an appropriate place. Of course, if you don't know how you made it in the first place, this can present some difficulties!

I'LL FIX THAT LATER

Minor disasters do tend to get out of hand if you put them away till later. They multiply and breed in the cupboard and wait to be discovered several seasons later . . . probably when you are stuffing another minor disaster in the same cupboard. Do not despair. You are not alone in this experience. Take consolation in the knowledge of the story of 'The Princess and the Scissors'. You may have heard a different version of the same story, 'The Princess and the Pea'. The true origin of the story, (and I challenge you to disprove it) has a princess sleeping on the queen's minor disasters, not on layers of mattresses. And the object that caused great discomfort to the princess was actually a pair of scissors and not a pea. This is so much more likely, don't you think? Take heart and continue reading about 'fixing' knitting with this added sense of history behind you.

REKNITTING UP LADDERS

A crochet hook is an asset if you do not wish to keep a ladder in your design. If more than one stitch has laddered, hold all the stitches except the one you are working on with a cable needle or safety pin. To correct a knitwise ladder, insert a crochet hook through the front of the dropped stitch. Hook up the lowest bar and pull it through the loop to form a new stitch. Do the same for the next lowest bar, continuing up to the level of the knitting needles. If, after hooking up to the top, there is an extra bar remaining, don't panic. It won't go anywhere if it is left. You may wish to allow the stitch to ladder back to the bar and try picking it up again.

The hooking technique outlined above can be deliberately used to create a false seam in circular knitting. Hook two bars at once, then one on its own, then two, and so on. This raises and stabilises a line down the knitting. It is quite useful should you wish to shorten a garment without actually cutting off any of it. Simply hook two bars together each time, gathering a vertical line and creating a scalloped edge.

IF THE GARMENT IS TOO BIG

There is actually no such thing as a jersey that is too big! It will simply have loose cuffs and bands. By making these fit you will have a "comfortable favourite" garment. To undertake the operation you will need one of the following sets of equipment.

° Thonging cord to thread through the waist, cuffs and body of the garment and gather it down to a more manageable size.
° Invisible knitting elastic, hat elastic or shirring elastic to thread through the welts of the garment if it requires only minor adjustment. Use a wool needle to thread the elastic through the bottom edge and the top of the band. Also thread elastic through the middle rows of the band as many times as necessary to give it enough stretch. (It may not be necessary to put elastic through every row.)

° Shirring or flat elastic to gather up the length of the sleeves, as illustrated.
° Consider, too, using a combination of these techniques. See also the section on machine sewing on the next page.

TOO LONG AND SKINNY

If the original garment was simply too long and skinny, chop off the bottom and adjust it by cutting and pulling a thread and knitting on new ribbing. You may want to make it into a small waist-length garment or one with long ribbing reaching back to the original length. Try using the cut-off piece as the beginning of a new garment (it needn't necessarily form the bottom, either).

DRAMATIC SURGERY

For this process you'll need scissors, fine knitting needles and matching yarn, if available.

There are two methods of getting rid of a large section at the bottom of a garment.

For multi-coloured intarsia work or garments made from very fluffy or uneven wool: First, undo the side seams, leaving the front and back of the garment free. Mark the line that is to form the new level for the top of the band and cut the knitting several rows lower down. Unravel the knitting to the marked line and pick up the stitches on fine needles. Reknit the bands using the appropriate-sized needles.

For garments knitted from plain or evenly spun wools: Undo the side seams. Mark the place that is to form the new level for the top of the band, pull a thread and snip it off. The knitting will fall into two pieces. If necessary, unravel one further row to yield some wool for a new sewing up thread. Pick up the stitches using a smaller needle than that used for the original knitting, and reknit the bands.

To reknit a ribbed band only: Pull out and cut the thread forming the first row of

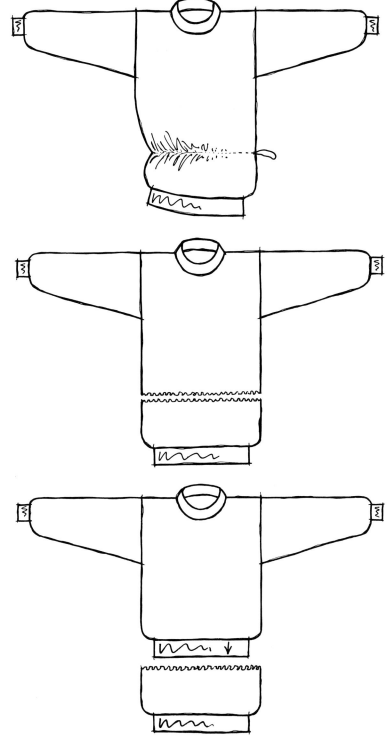

stocking stitch above the band. Pick up the stitches and rib downwards tightly, or decrease several stitches across the bottom of the knitting, then knit new ribbing.

You can use leftover pieces of ribbing as patches for sleeves or shoulder pads, and for many other purposes!

MACHINE SEWN ADJUSTMENTS

Major alterations can be made to the shape and size of a garment by bringing the sewing machine into the action. For the first two options outlined below, a sewing pattern is a great help in restyling sleeve tops and armhole shapings. A sewing pattern is also valuable when reshaping a raglan sleeve, although this is more straightforward. It is useful to remember that the back of a garment body is wider from armhole edge to armhole edge than the front. The number of stitches decreased for the beginning of the armhole is usually fewer on the back than the front of the garment.

Three methods of taking in a garment with set-in sleeves that is too big all over are outlined below.

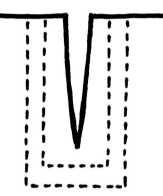

Machining and hand sewing the garment First, undo the side seams and armhole seams, take out the sleeves and unpick the sleeve seams. With a sewing machine, sew two straight lines of stitching one stitch apart where you require the new seams, one marking the placement of the new seam and one acting as stay stitching to reinforce the knitting and stop it unravelling. Baste the garment together and try it on. If it fits, trim off the excess knitting bravely. Sew the garment together by hand using the bar-to-bar front-facing method (see Chapter 7, Finishing), hiding the machine basting just inside the seam.

Machining the entire alteration Remove the sleeves, but don't undo the sleeve seams or side seams of the garment. With the garment inside out, baste new

seam lines on the body part. Baste a new placement line for the set-in sleeves. Baste the new seam line on the sleeve top, taking into account any adjustments needed to fit the sleeve top into the new sleeve opening. Try on the garment while it is still inside out, with the sleeves set in (this is to make sure that nothing horribly irreversible is about to happen!).

Remove the sleeves. Take off the garment and machine sew the new side seams with two rows of straight stitching through both layers, as in ordinary machine sewing. Reshape and sew the new lines for the sleeve shaping on the body of the garment, again using two lines of straight stitching. Reshape and sew the new sleeve top lines with two lines of straight stitching.

Sew new sleeve seams from armhole to cuff by sewing two lines of straight stitching as outlined above. Trim off the excess knitting. Reset the sleeves and baste them in. Try on the garment, this time with the right side out. If all is well, sew the new armhole seam line on the machine. Any excess area in the sleeve top may be gathered to create a puff or may be evenly distributed around the armhole edge, with a little more puffing at the back and the top than at the front of the sleeve top.

Restyling the garment shape If the garment is absolutely huge and has set-in sleeves, it may be possibe to make it into a smaller dolman sleeve garment or off-the-shoulder style.

Lay out the garment inside out. For a dolman sleeve, pin and baste the new seam lines, starting from the bottom of the bands and gently curving all the way to the cuffs. The entire depth of the armhole will need

to be used. For an off-the-shoulder style the new underarm position will be well inside the original body part of the garment. In both cases the cuff needs to be tight to hold up the extra length in the sleeve top. If the original cuffs are loose, cut them off (you'll probably have to cut off about half the original sleeve) and pick up the stitches and knit new cuffs. If you do intend to knit new cuffs in this manner, cut off the bottoms of the sleeves before trimming the excess knitting off the sleeve seams. Then you can unravel the old cuffs and sleeve bottoms and use the yarn for the new cuffs.

You may wish to knit contrasting cuffs and reknit the neck with the same contrasting yarn. Here are some ideas for inventive alterations to necks.

° Knit a spiky strip of moss or garter stitch, with one edge straight and one edge pointed in a random or patterned manner. This may be done by constantly increasing and decreasing stitches as the collar is knitted. It would fit best onto a wide curved neck or boat neck rather than a crew or V neck.

° Add feathers or beading to the neckline.

° Make a knitted yolk on circular needles, incorporating textured yarn or ribbon banding (see Chapter 8, Embellishments).

If the body of the garment was originally very wide you could make new knitted sleeves that reflect the new line of the neck, tying the whole design together. They will appear as large decorative cuffs because the original armhole line will probably reach to the elbow in the new garment.

IF THE GARMENT IS TOO SMALL

If one of your creations simply doesn't fit the intended owner, the most obvious solution is to find a new and caring home for it. Alternatively, try blocking and stretching the garment or adding pieces where required. The easiest styles to alter by adding pieces are drop-shouldered garments.

Undo the side seams and knit new strips to be joined to the sides. If you like, eliminate the side seams by knitting strips that reach right around from the front to the back edges of the original knitting. When you reach the point for the armhole opening, split the knitting by transferring half the stitches onto a stitch holder. (Remember that drop shouldered garments need quite deep armholes.) Continue knitting on one set of stitches until the new piece is the right length. Join the yarn to the remaining set of stitches and complete that side to match. To add width to a sleeve, simply flip it over so the seam is facing up. Undo the seam and add a knitted strip.

It is not necessary to knit

such strips in the same direction as the original knitting. Stitches may be picked up sideways from the side or sleeve seams. If the strip is to be knitted with the same needles and yarn, simply use

the body of the garment as a tension sample and count the number of stitches and rows per 10 cm.

Because of the rectangular shape of the knitted stitch, the number of rows up the side

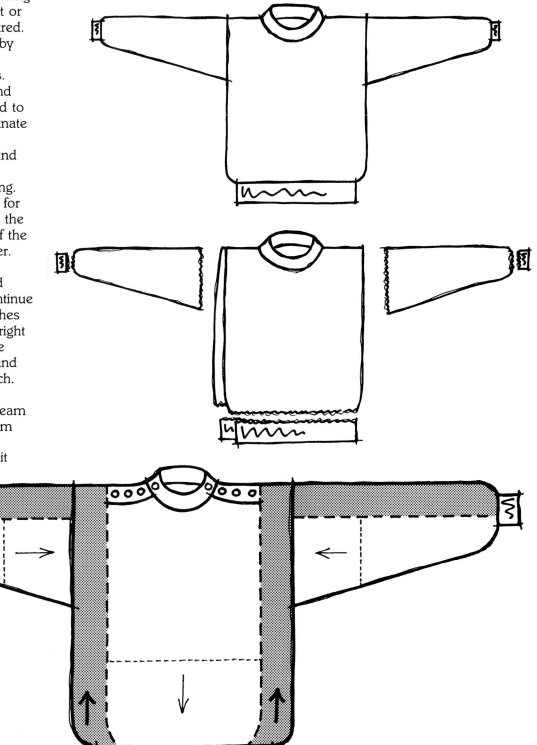

seams probably will not correspond with the number of stitches required to knit a sideways strip in the same tension. Usually, fewer stitches are required for the strip. If you picked up one stitch for every row it is likely that the new knitting would form a frill radiating out from the side seam. Of course, you may wish to utilise this technique, deliberately using a very fine yarn and picking up extra stitches to create a ruched effect for the side panels. If different yarns have been used on the new side or sleeve panels, consider tying the design together further by including them in a new neckline.

A neck opening that is too small to go over the head or is uncomfortably tight is not an uncommon occurrence. Several cures are outlined here.

If the neckline is a crew or polo neck that has been knitted on ordinary straight needles, open the side seam, turn down the collar and let it hang open. Alternatively, if it feels comfortable once it is over the head, add a loop and a button so it may be worn closed.

If, after opening the side seam, the neck opening is still too small, try opening one shoulder. To keep out draughts in a woolly winter garment, add knitted bands to both edges of the shoulder opening. Work buttonholes in the front shoulder band and sew buttons to the back shoulder band.

Further adjustments may be necessary if the neckline feels uncomfortable, despite opening the neck and one shoulder seam. If this is the case, undo the other shoulder seam and unravel the neckline

down to the beginning of the neck shaping. Pick up the stitches and reknit the neckline to make the opening wider. You may have to add extra length to the neck to make the opening large enough. Remember to reknit the back neck to correspond with the new front neck shaping, and reset the sleeves if necessary.

To make a garment longer, remove the bands by cutting and pulling a thread from the row immediately above the bands. Pick up the stitches and knit down to the required length. Provided the width of the garment remains the same, graft the ribbing onto the new knitting, as outlined in Chapter 4, Measuring and mechanics. This technique is useful for invisibly removing and replacing an offending section of the work.

Author's note
It is now seven years since the first publication of this book. I hope this fourth printing encourages a new batch of adventurous knitters and reminds the others to continue to stretch.

Thank you to Trace Hodgson of Wellington, New Zealand for the wonderful cartoons in this book, including the cover.

All the technical drawings were done by Barbara Henderson whom we all miss.

THE NEW ZEALAND SPINNING, WEAVING AND WOOLCRAFTS COUNCIL

The N.Z. Spinning, Weaving and Woolcrafts Council was set up "to foster interest in, develop and promote the spinning, weaving, knitting and dyeing of wool and other fibres and all other crafts pertaining to the uses of wool and other fibres". Among its many activities, the council organises national and overseas exhibitions and provides information to is members. Its magazine, *The Web,* may be obtained from the Editor, Miss Yvonne Davidson, P.O. Box 233, Greymouth. Membership applications should be made to the Secretary, Mrs Gwen Stacy, 5 Mallam Street, Wellington 5.

THE CRAFTS COUNCIL OF NEW ZEALAND INC.

The Crafts Council of New Zealand Inc. is recognised as the national body of crafts people in New Zealand. It produces the magazine *New Zealand Craft,* which contains letters, articles, photographs, national and international exhibition dates and events. A newsletter between magazines keeps crafts people informed of the council's activities. The council also has a gallery in Wellington offering a wide variety of high quality New Zealand crafts. Collections of slides, books and information on craft throughout the world are available to members through the Resource Officer.

Membership applications can be obtained by writing to: Crafts Council of New Zealand Inc., P.O. Box 498, Wellington

A GUIDE TO NEW ZEALAND SHEEP

New Zealand Romney Have long,

medium-lustre wool that is used in carpets, overcoats, furnishings and handknitting yarns. Romneys can be found *everywhere!* (Have you checked your backyard recently?)

Merino Merinos can be found in the mountainous high country of the South Island. Their fine, highly crimped wool is used in handknitting yarns, baby clothes and other high quality apparel. The fineness of the wool comes from the high number of fibres — about 50 million compared to 15 million for the Romney!

Perendale The classic, hardy hill country sheep. There are over 11 million Perendales in

New Zealand and this is a breed especially developed for New Zealand's climate — it practically takes care of itself! Perendale wool has an exceptional spring to it which means that your handknitting yarn is full without the weight and springs back to shape if you stretch it.

New Zealand Halfbred Born of the cross between the Merino and other long-haired breeds, the New Zealand Crossbred wool is used for apparel and fine knitwear. This sheep can be found in the foothills of the South Island and in light rainfall areas (without its raincoat on . . .)

Drysdale It's not surprising that Drysdale wool goes into making carpets — this sheep looks like a walking carpet. Drysdale wool has very little crimp and this means that it is long and straight and shaggy — with just the strength for tough use in carpeting. The Drysdale was a genetic research experiment. Today it is widespread throughout New Zealand and very visible with its curving horns.